iOS Application Development with OpenCV 3

Create four mobile apps and explore the world through photography and computer vision

Joseph Howse

[PACKT] PUBLISHING

BIRMINGHAM - MUMBAI

iOS Application Development with OpenCV 3

First published: June 2016

Production reference: 1230616

Published by Packt Publishing Ltd.
Livery Place
35 Livery Street
Birmingham B3 2PB, UK.

ISBN 978-1-78528-949-1

www.packtpub.com

Credits

Author
Joseph Howse

Reviewer
Mohit Athwani

Commissioning Editor
Sarah Crofton

Acquisition Editor
Rahul Nair

Content Development Editor
Samantha Gonsalves

Technical Editor
Vivek Arora

Copy Editor
Tasneem Fatehi

Project Coordinator
Sanchita Mandal

Proofreader
Safis Editing

Indexer
Mariammal Chettiyar

Graphics
Disha Haria

Production Coordinator
Arvindkumar Gupta

Cover Work
Arvindkumar Gupta

About the Author

Joseph Howse lives in Canada. During the cold winters, he grows a beard and his four cats grow thick coats of fur. He combs the cats every day. Sometimes the cats pull his beard.

Joseph has been writing for Packt Publishing since 2012. His books include *OpenCV for Secret Agents*, *OpenCV 3 Blueprints*, *Android Application Programming with OpenCV 3*, *iOS Application Development with OpenCV 3*, *Learning OpenCV 3 Computer Vision with Python*, and *Python Game Programming by Example*.

When he is not writing books or grooming cats, Joseph provides consulting, training, and software development services through his company, Nummist Media (http://nummist.com/).

Acknowledgments

As always, Mom, Dad, and the cats have provided all kinds of support, including assistance with the photography in this book.

I am glad for this chance to recognize the iOS developers who trained me years ago. They include Alex Brodsky, Bill Wilson, Jesse Rusak, and Woody Lidstone.

During the writing of this book, I have benefitted from the opportunity to do other OpenCV projects with local colleagues such as Jeff Leadbetter, Matt Wright, Jad Tawil, and Kevin J. Gallant. I am proud that we are part of a growing computer vision community in Atlantic Canada.

Once again, the team at Packt Publishing has supported me with tremendous energy, skill, and loyalty. Thank you! Harsha Bharwani persuaded me to write another OpenCV book. After all, the set was incomplete without iOS. Samantha Gonsalves guided the project to completion, and she never let any complication discourage her or me. All the editors and the technical reviewer have added their marks of quality to the book, and have helped it speak to its audience. Please meet the technical reviewer by reading his biography here.

Finally, I want to thank my readers and the OpenCV community for the great years of learning that we have shared, and even greater years ahead!

About the Reviewer

Mohit Athwani is a self-taught iOS developer and has been developing apps since the early days of iOS 3. He has worked with several clients all around the world and has carried out intense research in the field of facial detection and recognition on iOS. His app, iRajanee, became the number one app on the Indian app store and fetched him tremendous success.

Mohit started his company, Geeks (http://www.geeksincorporated.net/), with a friend in 2010 and has since also involved himself in conducting training sessions on iOS for students and corporates alike. His website, http://indianios.guru/, hosts a lot of introductory videos and tutorials on developing for iOS with Swift.

I would like to thank my parents for gifting me my first MacBook and iPhone that allowed me to become an iOS developer. I would like to thank my friends and everybody who has encouraged me to come up with new ideas and concepts and I would also like to thank Packt Publishing for giving me the opportunity to review this book.

www.PacktPub.com

eBooks, discount offers, and more

Did you know that Packt offers eBook versions of every book published, with PDF and ePub files available? You can upgrade to the eBook version at www.PacktPub.com and as a print book customer, you are entitled to a discount on the eBook copy. Get in touch with us at customercare@packtpub.com for more details.

At www.PacktPub.com, you can also read a collection of free technical articles, sign up for a range of free newsletters and receive exclusive discounts and offers on Packt books and eBooks.

https://www2.packtpub.com/books/subscription/packtlib

Do you need instant solutions to your IT questions? PacktLib is Packt's online digital book library. Here, you can search, access, and read Packt's entire library of books.

Why subscribe?

- Fully searchable across every book published by Packt
- Copy and paste, print, and bookmark content
- On demand and accessible via a web browser

I dedicate my work to Sam, Jan, Bob, Bunny, and the cats,
who have been my lifelong guides and companions.

Table of Contents

Preface

Although iOS started as an operating system for a phone, it now fills a much broader role in a world of mobile and connected devices. Among their many functions, iOS devices act as smart cameras, offering a programmable imaging chain with a good set of features and optimizations in hardware and software. Moreover, iOS has great support for C and C++, which are the dominant languages of computer vision libraries. This point brings us to OpenCV, a cross-platform, open source, C++ library that provides optimized implementations of algorithms for computer vision, image processing, and machine learning. OpenCV has good iOS support, including functionality to bridge the differences between OpenCV's C++ types and iOS SDK's Objective-C types.

I began to work as an iOS and Android developer in 2010 and then as an OpenCV developer in 2012. The demand for these technologies has grown tremendously in just a few years. Ideas about low-cost smart cameras have captured the imagination of inventors and marketers, and OpenCV has proven to be a versatile library for rapidly prototyping these ideas. For me, this surge of interest in the field has provided opportunities to write technical books, found a business, and come in contact with fellow computer vision enthusiasts who live on every inhabited continent. People are building careers in computer vision everywhere — not just in the San Francisco Bay area but also in San Salvador, Kampala, Tehran, Bremen, and my home city of Halifax in Canada, to name just a few of the places where loyal readers live.

At the time of writing, this is the only book on OpenCV 3 for iOS, and it is much more extensive than any online tutorials on the subject. The book's code is tested with OpenCV 3.1, which offers many bug fixes and improvements compared to OpenCV 3.0. I hope this collection of sample applications and reference material makes the library more accessible to scholars, workers, and creators such as you!

What this book covers

Chapter 1, Setting Up Software and Hardware, covers the installation of an iOS development environment and OpenCV. To test our setup, we build a minimal application, CoolPig, which manipulates colors in a picture of a pig. Finally, we consider some photographic techniques and accessories.

Chapter 2, Capturing, Storing, and Sharing Photos, deals with camera control, the Photos library, and social networks. We build a photography app, LightWork.

Chapter 3, Blending Images, adds new features to our LightWork app. We use simple arithmetic operations as well as more complex filters to blend pairs of images in real time.

Chapter 4, Detecting and Merging Faces of Mammals, is about detection, classification, and geometric transformation, with an emphasis on faces. We create an application called ManyMasks, which can align and blend the faces of humans, cats, and possibly other mammals.

Chapter 5, Classifying Coins and Commodities, deals with detection and classification but with an emphasis on objects that have distinctive colors or designs. Our final application, BeanCounter, can classify coins, beans, and other objects, depending on a configuration file and a set of training images.

What you need for this book

You need a computer running Mac OS 10.10 (or a later version) as well as an iPhone, iPad, or iPod Touch running iOS 9 (or a later version).

On your computer, you need to install Apple's standard tools for iOS developers. These include Xcode, iOS SDK, and the Xcode Command Line Tools. You also need to set up OpenCV 3.1 (or a later version). All this software is free, and *Chapter 1, Setting Up Software and Hardware*, provides setup instructions.

Who this book is for

This book is great for developers who are new to iOS, computer vision, or both. Previous experience with Objective-C or C++ is recommended.

Conventions

In this book, you will find a number of text styles that distinguish between different kinds of information. Here are some examples of these styles and an explanation of their meaning.

Code words in text, database table names, folder names, filenames, file extensions, pathnames, dummy URLs, user input, and Twitter handles are shown as follows: "Next, let's define the instance variables of the `ViewController` class."

A block of code is set as follows:

```
- (void) startBusyMode {
  dispatch_async(dispatch_get_main_queue(), ^{
    [self.activityIndicatorView startAnimating];
    for (UIBarItem *item in self.toolbar.items) {
      item.enabled = NO;
    }
  });
}
```

Any command-line input or output is written as follows:

```
$ ./<opencv_source_path>/platforms/ios/build_framework.py
<opencv_contrib_build_path> --contrib <opencv_contrib_source_path>
```

New terms and **important words** are shown in bold. Words that you see on the screen, for example, in menus or dialog boxes, appear in the text like this: "Choose the **Value Changed** event, which occurs when the user selects a new option in the segmented control."

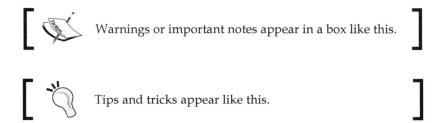

[Warnings or important notes appear in a box like this.]

[Tips and tricks appear like this.]

Reader feedback

Feedback from our readers is always welcome. Let us know what you think about this book—what you liked or disliked. Reader feedback is important for us as it helps us develop titles that you will really get the most out of.

To send us general feedback, simply e-mail feedback@packtpub.com, and mention the book's title in the subject of your message.

If there is a topic that you have expertise in and you are interested in either writing or contributing to a book, see our author guide at www.packtpub.com/authors.

Customer support

Now that you are the proud owner of a Packt book, we have a number of things to help you to get the most from your purchase.

Downloading the example code

You can download the example code files for this book from your account at http://www.packtpub.com. If you purchased this book elsewhere, you can visit http://www.packtpub.com/support and register to have the files e-mailed directly to you.

You can download the code files by following these steps:

1. Log in or register to our website using your e-mail address and password.
2. Hover the mouse pointer on the **SUPPORT** tab at the top.
3. Click on **Code Downloads & Errata**.
4. Enter the name of the book in the **Search** box.
5. Select the book for which you're looking to download the code files.
6. Choose from the drop-down menu where you purchased this book from.
7. Click on **Code Download**.

You can also download the code files by clicking on the **Code Files** button on the book's webpage at the Packt Publishing website. This page can be accessed by entering the book's name in the **Search** box. Please note that you need to be logged in to your Packt account.

Once the file is downloaded, please make sure that you unzip or extract the folder using the latest version of:

- WinRAR / 7-Zip for Windows
- Zipeg / iZip / UnRarX for Mac
- 7-Zip / PeaZip for Linux

Updated code for the book is also hosted on GitHub at `https://github.com/PacktPublishing/iOS-Application-Development-with-OpenCV3`. We also have other code bundles from our rich catalog of books and videos available at `https://github.com/PacktPublishing/`. Check them out!

Downloading the color images of this book

We also provide you with a PDF file that has color images of the screenshots/diagrams used in this book. The color images will help you better understand the changes in the output. You can download this file from `http://www.packtpub.com/sites/default/files/downloads/iOSApplicationDevelopmentwithOpenCV3_ColorImages.pdf`.

Errata

Although we have taken every care to ensure the accuracy of our content, mistakes do happen. If you find a mistake in one of our books — maybe a mistake in the text or the code — we would be grateful if you could report this to us. By doing so, you can save other readers from frustration and help us improve subsequent versions of this book. If you find any errata, please report them by visiting `http://www.packtpub.com/submit-errata`, selecting your book, clicking on the **Errata Submission Form** link, and entering the details of your errata. Once your errata are verified, your submission will be accepted and the errata will be uploaded to our website or added to any list of existing errata under the Errata section of that title.

To view the previously submitted errata, go to `https://www.packtpub.com/books/content/support` and enter the name of the book in the search field. The required information will appear under the **Errata** section.

Since this book has a GitHub repository, you can also report errata by creating an issue at `https://github.com/JoeHowse/iOSWithOpenCV/issues`.

Piracy

Piracy of copyrighted material on the Internet is an ongoing problem across all media. At Packt, we take the protection of our copyright and licenses very seriously. If you come across any illegal copies of our works in any form on the Internet, please provide us with the location address or website name immediately so that we can pursue a remedy.

Please contact us at copyright@packtpub.com with a link to the suspected pirated material.

We appreciate your help in protecting our authors and our ability to bring you valuable content.

Questions

If you have a problem with any aspect of this book, you can contact us at questions@packtpub.com, and we will do our best to address the problem.

You can also contact the author directly at josephhowse@nummist.com, or check his website, http://nummist.com/opencv, for answers to common questions about his books.

1
Setting Up Software and Hardware

Every year since 2007, the iPhone has spawned a new generation of hardware, and eager buyers have queued up outside their local Apple Store to get it. The iPhone and iPad have become centerpieces of consumer culture, promising instant gratification, timely information, and easy achievements. Apps are designed for retirees, working people, job hunters, vacationers, students, gamers, hospital patients, babies, and cats. Like a Swiss Army knife, an iPhone is a premium product that supposedly prepares the user for all kinds of contingencies. Moreover, the iPhone is a fashion item and sometimes inspires idiosyncratic behavior. For example, it enables the user to share large numbers of selfies and pictures of lunch.

As software developers and scholars of computer vision, we need to think a bit harder about the iPhone, the iPad, and their cameras. We need to make preparations before we can properly use these versatile tools in our work. We also need to demystify Apple's proprietary systems and appreciate the role of open source, cross-platform libraries such as OpenCV. Apple provides a fine mobile platform in iOS, but computer vision is not a fundamental part of this platform. OpenCV uses this platform efficiently but adds a layer of abstraction, providing high-level functionality for computer vision.

This chapter is the primer for the rest of the book. We assume that you already have a computer running Mac OS 10.10 (or a later version) as well as an iPhone, iPad, or iPod Touch running iOS 9 (or a later version). We will take the following steps to prepare a workspace and learn good habits for our future projects:

1. Set up Apple's standard tools for iOS developers, which include Xcode, iOS SDK, and Xcode Command Line Tools.

2. Set up OpenCV 3.1 (or a later version) for iOS. We have the option to use a standard, prebuilt version or a custom-built version with extra functionality.

3. Develop a minimal application that uses the iOS SDK and OpenCV to display an image with a special effect.

4. Join Apple's iOS Developer Program and obtaining permission to distribute an application to other users to test.

5. Find documentation and support for the iOS SDK and OpenCV.

6. Learn about the kinds of lights, tripods, and lens attachments that may enable us to capture specialized images with an iPhone or iPad.

By the end of this chapter, you will possess the necessary software and skills to build a basic OpenCV project for iOS. You will also have a new appreciation of your iPhone or iPad's camera as a tool for scientific photography and computer vision.

Setting up Apple's developer tools

The Xcode **integrated development environment** (IDE) is Apple's core product for developers. It includes GUI tools for the design, configuration, development, and testing of apps. As an add-on, the Xcode Command Line Tools enable full control of Xcode projects from the command prompt in Terminal. For iOS developers, the iOS SDK is also essential. It includes all the standard iOS libraries as well as tools for simulation and deployment.

Xcode is available for free from the Mac App Store and comes with the current version of the iOS SDK. Go to `https://itunes.apple.com/us/app/xcode/id497799835`, open Xcode's App Store link, and start the installer. The installer may run for an hour or longer, including the time to download Xcode and the iOS SDK. Give your agreement to any prompts, including the prompt to reboot.

Once Xcode is installed, open Terminal and run the following command to install the Xcode Command Line Tools:

```
$ xcode-select install
```

Again, give your agreement to any prompts. Once the Xcode Command Line Tools are installed, run the following command to ensure that you have reviewed and accepted the required license agreements:

```
$ sudo xcodebuild -license
```

The text of the agreements will appear in Terminal. Press spacebar repeatedly until you reach the end of the text, then type agree, and press *Enter*. Now, we have the basic tools to develop iOS projects in Xcode and Terminal.

Setting up the OpenCV framework

OpenCV for iOS is distributed as a framework file, which is a bundle containing the library's header files as well as binary files for static linkage. The binaries support all iOS device architectures (ARMv7, ARMv7s, and ARM64) and all iOS simulator architectures (x86 and x64). Thus, we can use the same framework file for all configurations of an iOS application project.

OpenCV 3 is designed to be modular. Its build process is highly configurable to allow modules to be added, reimplemented, or removed without breaking other modules. Each module consists of one public header file along with various private header files and implementation files. Some modules are considered standard components of an OpenCV build, and these standard modules are maintained and tested by the library's core development team. Other modules are considered extras, and these extra or "contributed" modules are maintained and tested by third-party contributors. Collectively, the extra modules are called opencv_contrib.

If we just want to use the standard modules, we can obtain the official, prebuilt distribution of OpenCV for iOS. This prebuilt distribution consists of a framework file, opencv2.framework. If we want to use extra modules, we must build opencv2.framework for ourselves. Next, let's examine the steps to get or build the framework.

 For this book's projects, the extra modules are not required but they are recommended because we will use them to implement some optional features.

Getting the prebuilt framework with standard modules

Go to http://opencv.org/downloads.html and click on the download link for the latest version of **OpenCV for iOS**. Specifically, we require OpenCV 3.1 or a later version. The download's filename is opencv2.framework.zip. Unzip it to get the framework file, opencv2.framework. Later, we will add this framework to our iOS application projects; we will import its header files using the following code:

```
#import <opencv2/core.hpp>
```

This imports the `core` module's header file from `opencv2.framework`. The import statement will vary according to the module's name.

Building the framework from source with extra modules

We will try to get and build all of OpenCV's modules. Broadly, this process will consist of the following four steps:

1. Get the source code for OpenCV's standard modules. Store this in any folder, which we will refer to as `<opencv_source_path>`.

2. Get the source code for OpenCV's extra modules. Store this in any folder, which we will refer to as `<opencv_contrib_source_path>`.

3. Try to build all the modules and store the build in any folder, which we will refer to as `<opencv_contrib_build_path>`.

4. If any module fails to build, resolve the issue by either removing the module or patching its source code. Then, try to build again.

Now, let's discuss the details as we walk through the steps. To obtain OpenCV's latest source code, we can use Git, an open source version control tool. We already installed Git as part of the Xcode Command Line Tools. OpenCV's standard and extra modules are hosted in two repositories on GitHub, an online repository hosting service. To download the standard modules' source code to `<opencv_source_path>`, run the following command:

```
$ git clone https://github.com/Itseez/opencv.git <opencv_source_path>
```

Similarly, to download the extra modules' source code to `<opencv_contrib_source_path>`, run the following command:

```
$ git clone https://github.com/Itseez/opencv_contrib.git <opencv_contrib_source_path>
```

 For an exhaustive guide to Git, see the book *Pro Git, 2nd Edition* (Apress, 2014) by Scott Chacon and Ben Straub. The free eBook version is available at https://www.git-scm.com/book.

OpenCV's source code comes with build scripts for various platforms. The iOS build script takes two arguments—the build path and the `opencv_contrib` source path. Run the script in the following manner:

```
$ ./<opencv_source_path>/platforms/ios/build_framework.py
<opencv_contrib_build_path> --contrib <opencv_contrib_source_path>
```

Read the script's output to see whether it failed to build any modules. Remember that `opencv_contrib` contains experimental modules from various authors, and some authors might not test their modules for iOS compatibility. For example, the following output shows a compilation error in the `saliency` module (`modules/saliency`):

```
** BUILD FAILED **


The following build commands failed:
  CompileC /Users/Joe/SDKs/OpenCV/fork_build_ios/build/iPhoneOS-armv7/
modules/saliency/OpenCV.build/Release-iphoneos/opencv_saliency_object.
build/Objects-normal/armv7/FilterTIG.o /Users/Joe/SDKs/OpenCV/fork_
contrib/modules/saliency/src/BING/FilterTIG.cpp normal armv7 c++ com.
apple.compilers.llvm.clang.1_0.compiler
(1 failure)
('Child returned:', 65)
```

If we do not require the problematic module, we may simply delete its source subfolder in `<opencv_contrib_source_path>/modules`, and then rerun `build_framework.py`. For example, to avoid building the `saliency` module, we may delete `<opencv_contrib_source_path>/modules/saliency`.

 For this book's projects, the following extra modules are useful:
- **xfeatures2d**: This provides extra algorithms to match images based on distinctive details in the images
- **xphoto**: This provides extra photo processing techniques

On the other hand, if we do require the problematic module, first somebody must modify its source code so that it successfully compiles and runs for iOS. Patching `opencv_contrib` is beyond the scope of this book, but if you are skilled in C++ programming, I encourage you to try it sometime. Alternatively, you may decide to file an issue report at `https://github.com/Itseez/opencv_contrib/issues` and wait for the module's authors to respond.

When `build_framework.py` works properly, it prints `** INSTALL SUCCEEDED **`, and creates the framework file at `<opencv_contrib_build_path>/opencv2.framework`. Later, we will add this framework to our iOS application projects; we will import its header files using the following code:

```
#import <opencv2/xphoto.hpp>
```

This imports the `xphoto` module's header file from `opencv2.framework`. The import statement will vary according to the module's name.

Making the extra modules optional in our code

As the extra modules are less stable than the standard modules, we may want to make them optional in our code. By enclosing the optional code inside a preprocessor condition, we can easily disable or re-enable it in order to test the effect. Consider the following example:

```
#ifdef WITH_OPENCV_CONTRIB
#import <opencv2/xphoto.hpp>
#endif
```

If we want to use `opencv2_contrib`, we will edit the Xcode project settings to add `WITH_OPENCV_CONTRIB` as a preprocessor definition. Then, in the preceding example, the `xphoto.hpp` headers will be imported in our code. Detailed steps to create a preprocessor definition are provided later in this chapter, in the *Configuring the project* section.

Developing a minimal application

So far, we have set up a development environment including Xcode, the iOS SDK, and OpenCV. Now, let's use these tools and libraries to develop our first iOS application. The app will have the following flow of execution:

1. When the application starts:
    1. Load an image from a file that is bundled with the app.
    2. If the image is in color (not grayscale), automatically adjust its white balance.
    3. Display the image in fullscreen mode.

2. Every two seconds:
    1. Create an updated image by applying a random tint to the original image.
    2. Display the updated image.

Note that the application will not use a camera or any user input at all. However, the user will see an image that appears to be backlit with a colorful, changing light. This is not really a demo of computer vision, but it is a demo of image processing and integration between the iOS SDK and OpenCV. Moreover, it is decorative, festive, and best of all it has a theme — *cool pigs*. Our app's name will be *CoolPig* and it will display a cool picture of a pig. Consider the following example of a black-and-white photo of a piglet (left), along with three tinted variants:

 In this book's print version, all images appear in grayscale. To see them in color, download them from Packt Publishing's website at `https://www.packtpub.com/sites/default/files/downloads/iOSApplicationDevelopmentwithOpenCV3_ColorImages.pdf`, or read the eBook.

The original image is the work of Gustav Heurlin (1862-1939), a Swedish photographer who documented rural life in the early 20th century. He was an early adopter of the autochrome color photography process, and *National Geographic* published many of his photographs during 1919-1931.

When our users see a pig in a beautiful series of pop-art colors, they will question their preconceptions and realize it is a really cool animal.

 To obtain the completed projects for this book, go to the author's GitHub repository at `https://github.com/JoeHowse/iOSWithOpenCV`, or log in to your account on Packt Publishing's site at `https://www.packtpub.com/`.

Creating the project

Open Xcode. Click on the **Create new Xcode project** button or select the **File | New | Project…** menu item. Now, a dialog asks you to choose a project template. Select **iOS | Application | Single View Application**, as shown in the following screenshot:

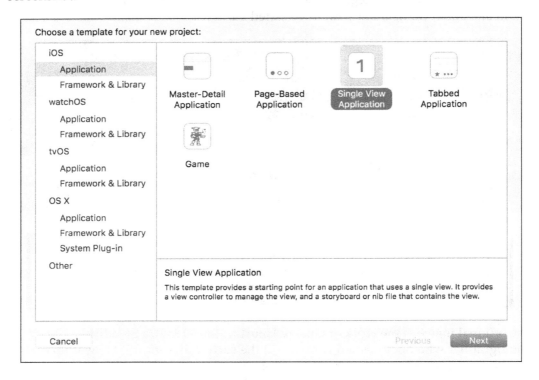

Single View Application is the simplest template as it just creates an empty GUI with no special navigational structure. Click on the **Next** button to confirm the selection. Now, a dialog asks you to pick a few project settings. Fill out the form as shown in the following screenshot:

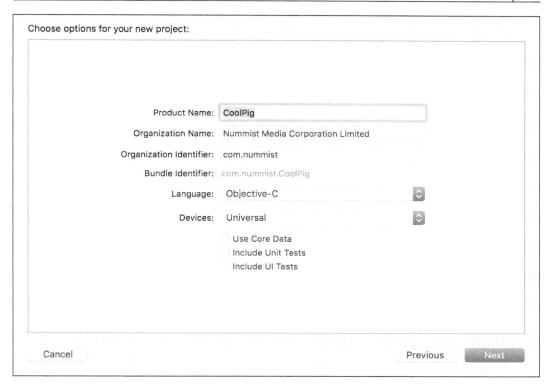

Choose options for your new project:

Product Name:	CoolPig
Organization Name:	Nummist Media Corporation Limited
Organization Identifier:	com.nummist
Bundle Identifier:	com.nummist.CoolPig
Language:	Objective-C
Devices:	Universal

Use Core Data
Include Unit Tests
Include UI Tests

Cancel   Previous   Next

Let's review the items in the form:

- **Product Name**: This is the application's name, such as CoolPig.

- **Organization Name**: This is the name of the application's vendor, such as Nummist Media Corporation Limited.

- **Organization Identifier**: This is the vendor's unique identifier. The identifier should use reverse domain name notation, such as com.nummist.

- **Bundle Identifier**: This is the application's unique identifier, which is generated based on the Product Name and Organization Identifier. This field is non-editable.

- **Language**: This is the project's high-level programming language, either **Objective-C** or **Swift**. This book uses Objective-C, which is a pure superset of C and interoperable with C++ to a great extent. Swift is not interoperable with C++. OpenCV's core language is C++, so Objective-C's interoperability makes it an obvious choice.

- **Devices**: This is the supported hardware, which may be **Universal** (all iOS devices), **iPhone** (including iPod Touch), or **iPad**. This book's projects are Universal.

- **Use Core Data**: If this is enabled, the project will contain a database using Apple's Core Data framework. For this book's projects, disable it.

- **Include Unit Tests**: If this is enabled, the project will contain a set of tests using the OCUnit framework. For this book's projects, disable it.

- **Include UI Tests**: If this is enabled, the project will contain a set of tests using Apple's UI automation framework for iOS. Disable it for this book's projects.

Click on the **Next** button to confirm the project options. Now, a file chooser dialog asks you to pick a folder for the project. Pick any location, which we will refer to as `<app_project_path>`.

Optionally, you may enable the **Create Git repository** checkbox if you want to put the project under version control using Git. Click on the **Create** button. Now, Xcode creates and opens the project.

Adding files to the project

Use Finder or Terminal to copy files to the following locations:

- `<app_project_path>/opencv2.framework`: This framework contains the standard OpenCV modules. We downloaded or built it previously, as described in the *Getting the prebuilt framework with standard modules* or *Building the framework from source with extra modules* section.

- `<app_project_path>/CoolPig/Piggy.png`: This may be any cool picture of a pig in grayscale or color. Any species of pig is acceptable, be it a swine, boar, Muppet, or other variety.

Go back to Xcode to view the project. Navigate to the **File** | **Add Files to "CoolPig"...** menu item. Now, Xcode opens a file chooser dialog. Select `opencv2.framework` and click on the **Add** button. Repeat the same steps for `CoolPig/Piggy.png`. Note that these files appear in the project navigator pane, which is the leftmost section of the Xcode window. In this pane, drag `Piggy.png` to the **CoolPig** | **Supporting Files** group. When you are finished, the navigator pane should look similar to the following screenshot:

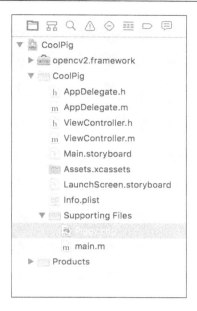

Configuring the project

First, let's configure our app to run in fullscreen mode with no status bar. Select the **CoolPig** project file at the top of the navigator pane. Now, select the **General** tab in the editor area, which is the central part of the Xcode window. Find the **Deployment Info** group, and enable the **Hide status bar** and **Requires full screen** checkboxes, as shown in the following screenshot:

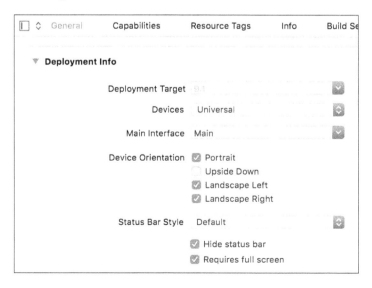

The status bar and fullscreen settings are stored in the app's `Info.plist` file. Select **CoolPig | CoolPig | Info.plist** in the navigator pane. Now, in the editor area, note that the **UIRequiresFullscreen** and **Status bar is initially hidden** properties both have the **YES** value. However, we still need to add another property to ensure that the status bar will not appear. Hover over the last item in the list, and click on the **+** button to insert a new property. Enter **View controller-based status bar appearance** as the property's key and set its value to **NO**, as shown in the following screenshot:

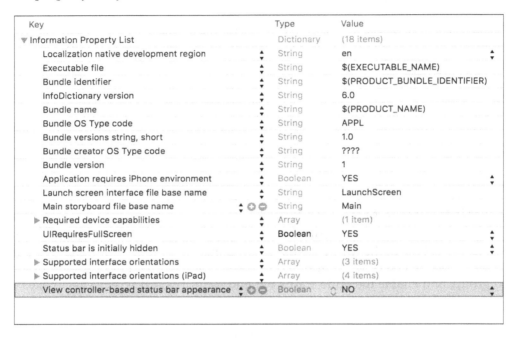

Key		Type	Value	
▼ Information Property List		Dictionary	(18 items)	
Localization native development region	‡	String	en	‡
Executable file	‡	String	$(EXECUTABLE_NAME)	
Bundle identifier	‡	String	$(PRODUCT_BUNDLE_IDENTIFIER)	
InfoDictionary version	‡	String	6.0	
Bundle name	‡	String	$(PRODUCT_NAME)	
Bundle OS Type code	‡	String	APPL	
Bundle versions string, short	‡	String	1.0	
Bundle creator OS Type code	‡	String	????	
Bundle version	‡	String	1	
Application requires iPhone environment	‡	Boolean	YES	‡
Launch screen interface file base name	‡	String	LaunchScreen	
Main storyboard file base name	‡ ⊕ ⊖	String	Main	
▶ Required device capabilities	‡	Array	(1 item)	
UIRequiresFullScreen	‡	Boolean	YES	‡
Status bar is initially hidden	‡	Boolean	YES	‡
▶ Supported interface orientations	‡	Array	(3 items)	
▶ Supported interface orientations (iPad)	‡	Array	(4 items)	
View controller-based status bar appearance	‡ ⊕ ⊖	Boolean	NO	‡

Next, let's link the project with additional frameworks. OpenCV depends on two of Apple's frameworks called `CoreGraphics.framework` and `UIKit.framework`. Optionally, for optimizations, OpenCV can also use a third Apple framework called `Accelerate.framework`.

> The Accelerate framework contains Apple's hardware-accelerated implementation of industry-standard APIs for vector mathematics. Notably, it implements standards called **Basic Linear Algebra Subprograms (BLAS)** and **Linear Algebra Package (LAPACK)**. OpenCV is designed to leverage these standards on various platforms including iOS.

Select the **CoolPig** project file in the navigator pane and then select the **Build Phases** tab in the editor area. Find the **Link Binary With Libraries** group. Click on the **+** button, select `Accelerate.framework` from the dialog, and click on the **Add** button. Repeat these steps for `CoreGraphics.framework` and `UIKit.framework`. Now, the editor area should look similar to the following screenshot:

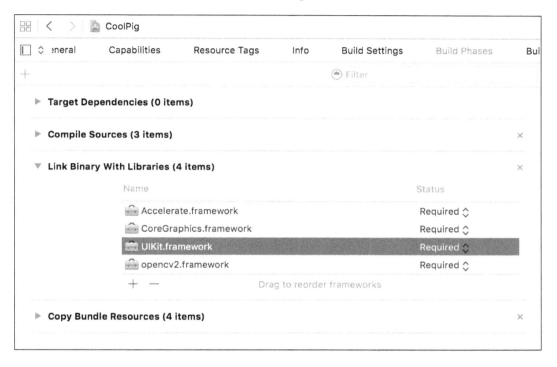

Now, the linker will be able to find OpenCV's dependencies. However, we need to change another setting to ensure that the compiler will understand the C++ code in OpenCV's header files. Open the **Build Settings** tab in the editor area and find the **Apple LLVM 7.0 - Language** group. Set the value of the **Compile Sources As** item to **Objective-C++**, as seen in the following screenshot:

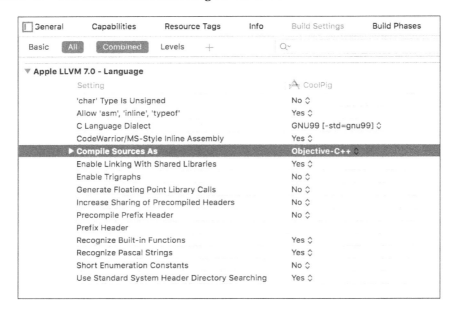

 Alternatively, we could leave the **Compile Sources As** item at its default value, which is **According to File Type**. Then, we would need to rename our source files to give them the extension .mm, which Xcode associates with Objective-C++.

We have just one more thing to configure in the **Build Settings** tab. Remember that we consider the opencv2_contrib modules to be an optional dependency of our projects, as described earlier in the *Making the extra modules optional in our code* section. If we did build opencv2.framework with these modules and if we do want to use their functionality, let's create a preprocessor definition, WITH_OPENCV_CONTRIB. Find the **Apple LLVM 7.0 - Preprocessing** group. Edit **Preprocessor Macros | Debug** and **Preprocessor Macros | Release** to add the WITH_OPENCV_CONTRIB text. Now, the settings should look like the following screenshot:

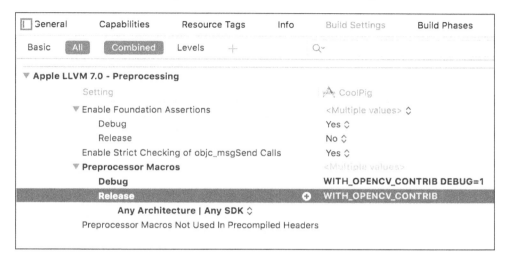

As a final, optional step in the configuration, you may want to set the app's icon. Select **CoolPig | CoolPig | Assets.xcassets** in the project navigator pane. **Assets.xcassets** is a bundle, which may contain several variants of the icon for different devices and different contexts (the Home screen, Spotlight searches, and the Settings menu).

Click on the **AppIcon** list item in the editor area and then drag and drop an image file into each square of the **AppIcon** grid. If the image's size is incorrect, Xcode will notify you so that you may resize the image and try again. Once you have added your images, the editor area might look similar to the following screenshot:

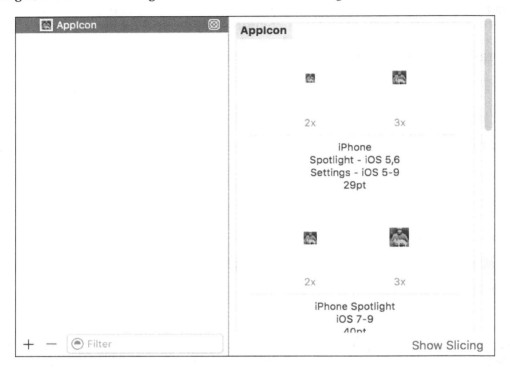

Laying out an interface

Now, our project is fully configured and we are ready to design its graphical user interface (GUI). Xcode comes with a built-in tool called Interface Builder, which enables us to arrange GUI elements, connect them to variables and events in our code, and even define the transitions between **scenes** (or informally, *screens*). Remember that CoolPig's GUI is just a fullscreen image. However, even our simple GUI has a transition between a static loading screen (where the image does not change color) and dynamic main screen (where the image changes color every two seconds). Let's first configure the loading screen and then the main screen.

Select **CoolPig | CoolPig | LaunchScreen.storyboard** in the navigator pane. This file is a **storyboard**, which stores the configuration of a set of scenes (or a single scene in this case). A scene hierarchy appears in the editor area. Navigate to **View Controller Scene | View Controller | View**. A blank view appears on the right-hand side of the editor area, as seen in the following screenshot:

Let's add an image view inside the empty view. Notice the list of available GUI widgets in the lower-right corner of the Xcode window. This area is called the **library pane**. Scroll through the library pane's contents. Find the **Image View** item and drag it to the empty view. Now, the editor area should look like this:

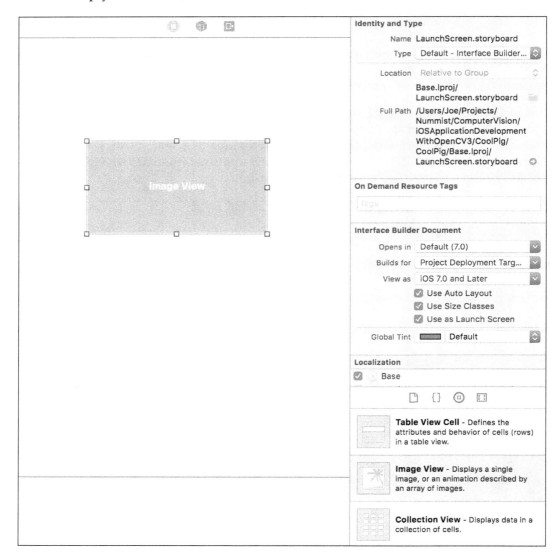

Drag the corners of the highlighted rectangle to make the image view fill its parent view. The result should look like this:

We still need to take a further step to ensure that the image view scales up or down to match the screen size on all devices. Click on the **Pin** button in the toolbar at the bottom of the editor area. The button's icon looks like a rectangle pinned between two lines. Now, a pop-up menu appears with the title **Add New Constraints**. Constraints define a widget's position and size relative to other widgets.

Specifically, we want to define the image view's margins relative to its parent view. To define a margin on every side, click on the four I-shaped lines that surround the square. They turn red. Now, enter 0 for the top and bottom values and -20 for the left and right values. Some iOS devices have built-in horizontal margins, and our negative values ensure that the image extends to the screen's edge even on these devices. The following screenshot shows the settings:

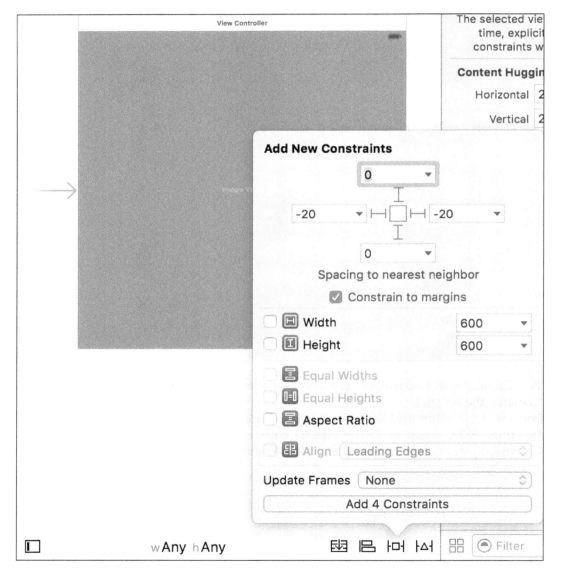

Click on the **Add 4 Constraints** button to confirm these parameters.

Finally, we want to show an image! Look at the inspector pane, which is in the top-right area of the Xcode window. Here, we can configure the currently selected widget. Select the **Attributes** tab. Its icon looks like a slider. From the **Image** drop-down list, select `Piggy.png`. From the **Mode** drop-down list, select **Aspect Fill**. This mode ensures that the image will fill the image view in both dimensions, without appearing stretched. The image may appear cropped in one dimension. Now, the editor area and inspector pane should look similar to the following screenshot:

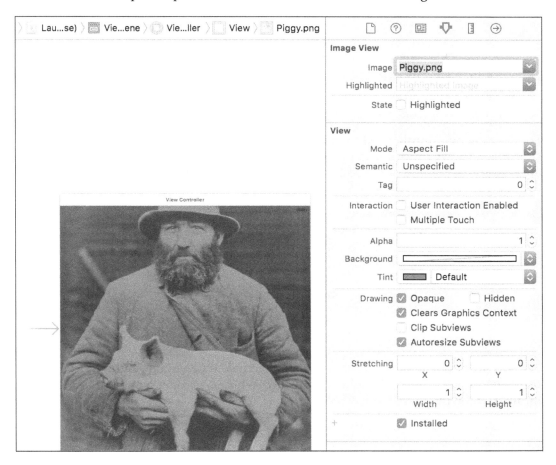

So far, we have completed the loading screen's layout. Now, let's turn our attention to the main screen. Select **CoolPig | CoolPig | Main.storyboard** in the project navigator. This storyboard, too, has a single scene. Select its view. Add an image view and configure it in exactly the same way as the loading screen's image view. Later, in the *Connecting an interface element to the code* section, we will connect this new image view to a variable in our code.

Writing the code

As part of the Single View Application project template, Xcode has already created the following code files for us:

- AppDelegate.h: This defines the public interface of an AppDelegate class. This class is responsible for managing the application's life cycle.

- AppDelegate.m: This contains the private interface and implementation of the AppDelegate class.

- ViewController.h: This defines the public interface of a ViewController class. This class is responsible for managing the application's main scene, which we saw in Main.Storyboard.

- ViewController.m: This contains the private interface and implementation of the ViewController class.

For CoolPig, we simply need to modify ViewController.m. Select **CoolPig | CoolPig | ViewController.m** in the project navigator. The code appears in the editor area. At the beginning of the code, let's add more #import statements to include the header files for several OpenCV modules, as seen in the following code:

```
#import <opencv2/core.hpp>
#import <opencv2/imgcodecs/ios.h>
#import <opencv2/imgproc.hpp>

#ifdef WITH_OPENCV_CONTRIB
#import <opencv2/xphoto.hpp>
#endif

#import "ViewController.h"
```

We will need to generate random numbers to create the image's random tint. For convenience, let's define the following macro, which generates a 64-bit floating-point number in the range of 0 to 1:

```
#define RAND_0_1() ((double)arc4random() / 0x100000000)
```

 The arc4random() function returns a random 32-bit integer in the range of 0 to 2^32-1 (or 0x100000000). The first time it is called, the function automatically seeds the random number generator.

The remainder of `ViewController.m` deals with the private interface and implementation of the `ViewController` class. Elsewhere, in `ViewController.h`, the class is declared as follows:

```
@interface ViewController : UIViewController
@end
```

Note that `ViewController` is a subclass of `UIViewController`, which is an important class in the iOS SDK. `UIViewController` manages the life cycle of a set of views and provides reasonable default behaviors as well as many methods that may override these defaults. If we develop applications according to the **model-view-controller (MVC)** pattern, then `UIViewController` is the controller or coordinator, which enforces good separation between the platform-specific view or GUI and platform-independent model or "business logic".

Let's turn our attention back to the private interface of `ViewController` in `ViewController.m`. The class keeps the original image and updated image as member variables. They are instances of OpenCV's `cv::Mat` class, which can represent any kind of image or other multidimensional data. `ViewController` also has a reference to the image view where we will display the image. Another of the class's properties is an `NSTimer` object, which will fire a callback every two seconds. Finally, the class has a method, `updateImage`, which will be responsible for displaying a new random variation of the image. Here is the code for `ViewController`'s private interface:

```
@interface ViewController () {
  cv::Mat originalMat;
  cv::Mat updatedMat;
}

@property IBOutlet UIImageView *imageView;
@property NSTimer *timer;

- (void)updateImage;

@end
```

Now, let's implement the methods of the ViewController class. It inherits many methods from its parent class, UIViewController, and we could override any of these. First, we want to override the viewDidLoad method, which runs when the scene is loaded from its storyboard. Typically, this is an appropriate time to initialize the view controller's member variables. Our implementation of viewDidLoad will begin by loading Piggy.png from file and converting it to OpenCV's RGB format. If the image was not originally grayscale and OpenCV's extra photo module is available, we will use a function from this module to adjust the white balance. Finally, we will start a timer to invoke our updateImage method every two seconds. Here is our code for viewDidLoad:

```
@implementation ViewController

- (void)viewDidLoad {
  [super viewDidLoad];

  // Load a UIImage from a resource file.
  UIImage *originalImage =
      [UIImage imageNamed:@"Piggy.png"];

  // Convert the UIImage to a cv::Mat.
  UIImageToMat(originalImage, originalMat);

  switch (originalMat.type()) {
    case CV_8UC1:
      // The cv::Mat is in grayscale format.
      // Convert it to RGB format.
      cv::cvtColor(originalMat, originalMat,
          cv::COLOR_GRAY2RGB);
      break;
    case CV_8UC4:
      // The cv::Mat is in RGBA format.
      // Convert it to RGB format.
      cv::cvtColor(originalMat, originalMat,
          cv::COLOR_RGBA2RGB);
#ifdef WITH_OPENCV_CONTRIB
      // Adjust the white balance.
      cv::xphoto::autowbGrayworld(originalMat,
          originalMat);
#endif
      break;
    case CV_8UC3:
```

```
        // The cv::Mat is in RGB format.
#ifdef WITH_OPENCV_CONTRIB
        // Adjust the white balance.
        cv::xphoto::autowbGrayworld(originalMat, originalMat);
#endif
        break;
    default:
        break;
    }

    // Call an update method every 2 seconds.
    self.timer = [NSTimer scheduledTimerWithTimeInterval:2.0
        target:self selector:@selector(updateImage)
        userInfo:nil repeats:YES];
}
```

 NSTimer only fires callbacks when the app is in the foreground. This behavior is convenient for our purposes because we only want to update the image when it is visible.

Now, let's implement the `updateImage` helper method. It will multiply each color channel by a random floating-point number. The following table describes the effects of multiplying various channels by a coefficient, *k*:

Value of k	Effect of multiplying red channel by k	Effect of multiplying green channel by k	Effect of multiplying blue channel by k
0 <= k < 1	Image becomes darker, with a cyan tint	Image becomes darker, with a magenta tint	Image becomes darker, with a yellow tint
k == 1	No change	No change	No change
k > 1	Image becomes brighter, with a red tint	Image becomes brighter, with a green tint	Image becomes brighter, with a blue tint

The following code generates the random color, multiplies it together with the original image, and displays the result in the image view:

```
- (void)updateImage {
  // Generate a random color.
  double r = 0.5 + RAND_0_1() * 1.0;
  double g = 0.6 + RAND_0_1() * 0.8;
  double b = 0.4 + RAND_0_1() * 1.2;
  cv::Scalar randomColor(r, g, b);

  // Create an updated, tinted cv::Mat by multiplying the
  // original cv::Mat and the random color.
  cv::multiply(originalMat, randomColor, updatedMat);

  // Convert the updated cv::Mat to a UIImage and display
  // it in the UIImageView.
  self.imageView.image = MatToUIImage(updatedMat);
}

@end
```

> Feel free to adjust the range of each random color coefficient to your taste. OpenCV clamps the result of the multiplication so that a color channel's value cannot overflow the 8-bit range of 0 to 255.

We have implemented all the custom logic of CoolPig in just 50 lines of code! The project template, storyboard, iOS SDK, and OpenCV provide many useful abstractions and thus enable us to focus on writing concise, application-specific code.

Connecting an interface element to the code

Let's connect the image view in Main.Storyboard to the imageView property in ViewController.m. Open Main.Storyboard in the project navigator, hold *command* and click on **View Controller** in the scene hierarchy. A dialog with a dark background appears. Right-click on the Piggy.png image view in the scene hierarchy and drag it to the circle beside **Outlets | imageView** in the dark dialog box, as shown in the following screenshot:

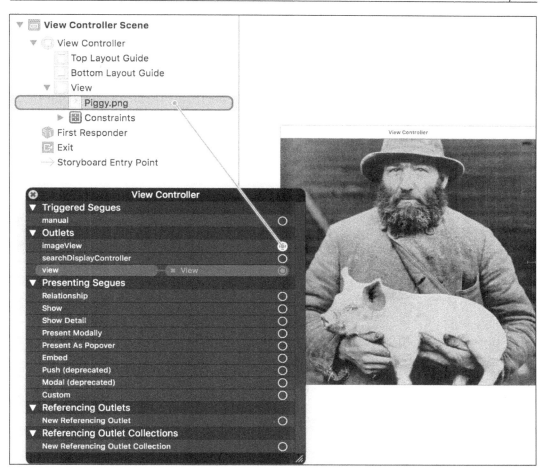

Release the mouse button to complete the connection. Close the dark dialog box.

Building and running the application

We are ready to build the app and run it in an iOS simulator or on an iOS device. First, if you want to use an iOS device, connect it to the Mac via a USB cable. The first time you connect a device, Xcode's top toolbar might show a progress bar and message, **Processing symbol files**. Wait for the message to disappear. Now, click on the **CoolPig** drop-down menu in Xcode's top toolbar and select the device or simulator that you want to use, such as **Devices | Joseph's iPad** or **iOS Simulators | iPad Pro**. Click on the **Run** button. Its icon is the standard triangular play symbol. Xcode builds the app, copies it to the device or simulator, and then launches it. Watch the pig change colors! For example, the app might look like this on an iPad Mini device:

 If you are using a simulator, you might find that its screen is too large to fit on your Mac's screen. To scale down the simulator's screen, go to the simulator's menu and select **Window | Scale | 50%** or another value.

Congratulations! We have built and run our first iOS application, including OpenCV for image processing and a pig for artistic reasons.

Distributing to testers and customers

Using the techniques we have learned thus far, we can build an app for iOS simulators and local iOS devices. For this, we do not require permission from Apple, and we do not need to purchase anything except a Mac for our development environment and any iOS devices for our testing.

On the other hand, if we want to distribute an app to other testers or publish it on the App Store, we must take a few more steps, spend a bit more money, and obtain permission from Apple. For details, see Apple's official App Distribution Guide at `https://developer.apple.com/library/ios/documentation/IDEs/Conceptual/AppDistributionGuide`. Briefly, a typical distribution process involves the following steps:

1. Enroll in the iOS Developer Program at `https://developer.apple.com/programs/enroll`. The cost of membership varies depending on where you live. It is $99 per year in the United States.

2. Optionally, use the iOS Provisioning Portal at `https://developer.apple.com/account` to create the credentials in order to distribute the app. Configure the Xcode project to use the credentials. Alternatively, Xcode may be able to create the credentials automatically even if you do not use the iOS Provisioning Portal.

3. Distribute your app to beta testers via Apple's TestFlight tools, which are part of the iTunes Connect tools at `https://itunesconnect.apple.com`.

4. If necessary, revise the app based on beta testers' feedback and retest.

5. Submit your app for publication via the iTunes Connect tools.

6. If necessary, revise the app based on Apple's feedback and resubmit.

7. Receive Apple's blessing and confirm that you are ready to release your app to the App Store. Reap the rewards of app publication!

Publishing an app (or a book!) is a significant undertaking and can be invigorating and humbling at the same time. Publication entails an ongoing responsibility to validate, fix, and promote your work and support your customers. This book's role is to impart valuable technical skills so that you can develop your own publishable projects in the field of computer vision!

Finding documentation and support

Outside this book, there is not much documentation or support on how to integrate OpenCV 3 into iOS projects. However, if you seek answers about OpenCV 3 in general or iOS in general, you will find a bigger community and a wealth of documentation. Consult the following sites:

- The official OpenCV documentation is available at http://docs.opencv.org. This includes tutorials as well as API docs.

- OpenCV Answers, the official Q&A site, is available at http://www.answers.opencv.org.

- Go to OpenCV's GitHub page at https://github.com/Itseez/opencv to find the latest source code, report issues, or contribute your own revisions. Similarly, see the extra modules' GitHub page at https://github.com/Itseez/opencv_contrib.

- The iOS Developer Library, including official documentation on Xcode and all the frameworks in the iOS SDK, is available at https://developer.apple.com/library/ios.

- The official iOS Developer Forum is located at https://devforums.apple.com/community/ios.

- StackOverflow (https://stackoverflow.com) is a Q&A community that includes many iOS developers and a few OpenCV developers.

- My website, http://nummist.com/opencv, is a good place to check for FAQ, errata, and updates pertaining to my books. Also check my GitHub repository for this book at https://github.com/JoeHowse/iOSWithOpenCV. Finally, feel free to e-mail me at josephhowse@nummist.com.

Understanding the camera and setting up photographic accessories

You have probably taken photos with an iOS device before. Perhaps you are even familiar with a variety of apps for image capture and image processing. Photography with an iPhone is certainly a popular pass time, and some people even define it as a distinct photographic movement called **iPhoneography**.

 If you are entirely new to iPhone photography, take some time now to try Apple's Camera and Photo apps, as well as some third-party photography apps.

iPhone users are not alone in espousing a brand-centric view of photography. For example, another movement called **Lomography** derives its inspiration from a film camera called the LOMO LC-A, released by the **Leningrad Optical Mechanical Associtaion (LOMO)** in 1984. LOMO makes precise optical instruments including microscopes, telescopes, night-vision devices, and medical imaging systems, but ironically the company entered the consumer market with a cheap and quirky camera. By conventional standards, the LC-A and its successors suffer from major optical and mechanical flaws, which result in blurry images with uneven brightness and coloration. Lomographers like the unconventional appearance of these images.

Likewise, iPhoneographers are not necessarily concerned with the predictability and fidelity (true-to-life quality) of the camera's images. Considering that a new iPhone costs between $450 and $750, many photographers would find its image quality disappointing and its controls very limited. It bears no resemblance to conventional cameras in the same price range. On the other hand, iPhoneographers may assign greater value to the iPhone's ability to capture photos discretely and edit and share them immediately.

Some users may crave the best of both worlds — the brains of an iPhone in the body of a slightly more conventional camera. There are many third-party photo accessories for iOS devices and these accessories mimic some of the components of a modular, professional photo system. Particularly, we will discuss three kinds of accessories: lighting, tripods, and lens attachments. To help us appreciate the purpose of these accessories, let's establish a baseline of comparison. The following table shows the specifications of the built-in lenses and image sensors in iOS devices' rear cameras:

Device	Resolution (pixels)	Sensor diagonal (mm)	Focal length (mm)	Diagonal FOV (degrees)	Maximum aperture
iPhone 4	2592x1936	5.68	3.85	72.8	f/2.8
iPhone 4S	3264x2448	5.68	4.28	67.1	f/2.4
iPhone 5, 5C	3264x2448	5.68	4.10	69.4	f/2.4
iPhone 5S	3264x2448	6.11	4.12	73.1	f/2.2
iPhone 6, 6 Plus	3264x2448	6.11	4.15	72.7	f/2.2
iPhone 6S, 6S Plus	4032x3024	6.11	4.15	72.7	f/2.2
iPad 3, 4	2592x1936	5.68	4.3	66.9	f/2.4
iPad Air 1 iPad Mini 1, 2, 3 iPod Touch 5	2592x1936	4.33	3.3	66.5	f/2.4
iPad Air 2 iPad Mini 4	3264x2448	4.61	3.3	69.9	f/2.4

The **field of view (FOV)** is the angle formed by the lens's focal point and two points at *diagonally* opposite edges of the visible space. Some authors may specify horizontal or vertical FOV instead of diagonal FOV. By convention, FOV implies diagonal FOV if not otherwise specified. The focal length is the distance between the image sensor and the lens's optical center when the lens is focused on an infinitely distant subject. See the following diagram:

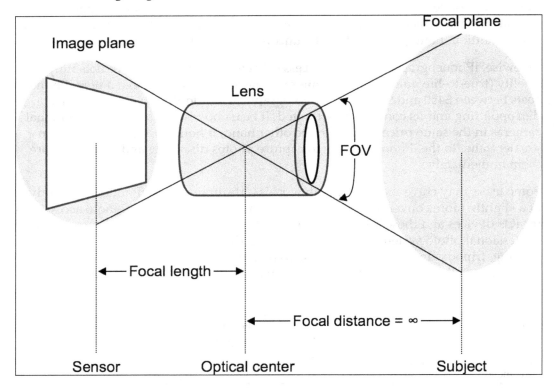

The diagonal FOV, the sensor's diagonal size, and the focal length are geometrically related according to the following formula:

```
diagonalFOVDegrees =
2 * atan(0.5 * sensorDiagonal / focalLength) * 180/pi
```

Depending on the model of the iOS device, the diagonal FOV ranges from 73.1 to 66.5 degrees. These values are equivalent to the FOV of a 29 mm to 33 mm lens in a traditional 35 mm camera system. Most photographers would characterize this FOV as *moderately wide*. Is moderately wide a good compromise? It depends on the use case. A wider angle helps to ensure that the subject literally has nowhere to hide. For example, this can be important in security applications. A narrower angle helps to ensure that details are captured even at a distance. For example, this can be important in product inspection applications, if the constraints of the workspace do not allow the camera to be placed close to the subject. If we want to choose the FOV, we must modify or accessorize the iOS device's optical system!

All the iOS cameras have small sensors. Their diagonal size ranges from 4.33 mm to 6.11 mm. For comparison, the diagonal size of the film or digital sensor in a 35 mm camera system is 43.3 mm. A smaller sensor has less capacity to gather light. To compensate, camera systems with small sensors tend to amplify the sensor's signal (the measurement of the light), but at the same time they amplify the random noise. Furthermore, to compensate for the noise, the system may blur the image. Thus, if we compare two images of the same scene at the same resolution, the image from the smaller sensor will tend to be noisier or blurrier. This difference becomes especially obvious when the light is dim. To summarize, we must expect that an iOS camera will take poor pictures in poor light. Thus, we must find or create good light!

Engineers may refer to the amplification of the sensor's signal as **gain** and photographers may refer to it as **ISO speed**. The latter metric is formally defined by the **International Standards Organization (ISO)**.

The ability to gather light is also directly related to the area of the lens's aperture. Typically, the aperture is expressed as an **f-number** or **f-stop**, which is defined as the ratio of the focal length to the aperture's diameter. Typically, an aperture is approximately circular and thus its area is proportional to the square of its radius. It follows that the intensity of the light passing through the aperture is inversely proportional to the square of the f-number. For example, an f/2 lens admits twice as much light as an f/2.8 lens. The iOS lenses have maximum apertures of f/2.2 to f/2.8, depending on the model. Values in this range are quite typical of wide-angle lenses in general, so the iOS lenses have neither an advantage nor disadvantage in this respect.

Finally, let's consider an issue of ergonomics. All iOS devices are lightweight and smooth and most of them are too small to hold in both hands. Thus, the user's grip is not firm. When a typical user holds out an iPhone to take a photo, the user's arm is like a long branch and the little iPhone shakes like a leaf. A high proportion of the pictures may suffer from motion blur. Comparatively, the design of a more traditional camera and lens may permit the user to brace the equipment's weight against his or her body in several places. Consider the following photograph:

The man in the background is Bob. Bob is left-handed. He is holding an iPhone in his left hand as he taps its camera button with his right hand. The man in the foreground is Joe. Joe is right-handed. He is equipped with a photo-sniper kit, which is a long lens mounted on two handles and a shoulder stock. The equipment's weight is braced against Joe's right knee and right shoulder. For additional stability, Joe's legs are folded and he is leaning leftward against a steel post and concrete slab. From another angle, the same pose looks like this:

This type of human stabilization can work well for some equipment. However, a more reliable approach is to use rigid support such as a tripod and we should definitely consider this when we tackle computer vision problems with a smartphone or tablet.

Now, let's take stock of the types of accessories that can change the lighting, stabilization, and perspective.

Lights

Many iOS devices have a built-in flash, which consists of a white LED light on the back of the device. Camera apps may activate the flash during photo capture, especially if the scene is dimly lit. Other apps may activate the flash for a long duration so that it acts as a flashlight or torch to help the user see. With only a single LED, the built-in flash may provide insufficient or uneven illumination in some circumstances.

If you need stronger or more evenly distributed illumination, or if your iOS device lacks a built-in flash altogether, you may want to purchase an external flash. Depending on the design, the external flash may mount as part of a case or may plug into the iOS device's audio jack. Typically, the external flash will have multiple white LEDs arranged in a line, grid, or ring. The latter design is called a **ring flash**.

Alternatively, in a controlled environment, you may set up any kind of lighting anywhere you please and you do not need to rely on the iOS device as a power source. Even a pair of well-placed desk lamps can greatly enhance the clarity and beauty of a scene. Normally, it is best to illuminate the subject from multiple angles to prevent shadows. Do not shine a light directly into the camera and do not illuminate the background more brightly than the subject, as these types of lighting tend to give the subject a very murky appearance with low contrast in the foreground. Sometimes, murky light can be artistically interesting, but it is not good for computer vision.

Tripods and other stabilization

A conventional photo camera has a threaded mount where the user may screw in the head of a tripod. Of course, an iOS device has no threaded mount. If we want to use a tripod with a standard screw, we may purchase an adapter that consists of a threaded mount and clip to hold the iOS device. Alternatively, we may purchase a tripod that has a built-in clip instead of a standard screw. Regardless of the type of mount, we also need to consider the following characteristics of the tripod:

*   **Height**: How tall is the tripod? Most tripods have extensible legs so that their height can vary. To help you decide what tripod height you require for a given application, consider how a person would normally look at the subject. If the subject is a small object such as a coin, a person might inspect it up close and similarly a short tripod might be appropriate. If the subject is a large object such as a lineup of cars on a highway, a person might watch it at eye level or might even look down on it from higher ground and similarly a tall tripod might be appropriate.

- **Weight**: A heavy tripod is cumbersome to carry, but it may be able to resist a destabilizing force such as a gust of wind.

- **Material**: Plastic may flex and crack. Metal may vibrate. Carbon fiber is less prone to these weaknesses, but it is relatively expensive. Some small tripods have bendable wire legs so that the user may wrap the tripod around another support, such as a branch or post. For example, GorillaPod is a well-known brand of tripods with bendable legs.

Typically, a small, lightweight tripod might cost between $10 and $30. This kind is often marketed as a mini or travel tripod. A tripod is a useful but optional accessory for all chapters in this book.

If you do not have a tripod or there is nowhere to place it, you may want to experiment with makeshift forms of stabilization. For example, if you want to monitor a room or hallway, you can tape the iOS device to a wall or ceiling. Be careful to choose tape that you can remove cleanly, without damaging the device's screen.

Lens attachments

A **lens attachment** or **add-on lens** is an additional optical unit that sits in front of the iPhone or iPad's built-in lens. Typically, the attachment is designed for the rear camera and its mount may consist of a magnet, clip, or case. The types of add-on lenses include the following:

- **Telephoto** attachment: This enables the lens to capture a narrower (zoomed in) field of view, comparable to a spyglass. Sometimes, a telephoto attachment is called a **zoom** attachment.

- **Wide-angle** attachment: This enables the lens to capture a wider (zoomed out) field of view.

- **Fisheye** attachment: This enables the lens to capture an extremely wide field of view, between 100 and 180 degrees diagonally. By design, the fisheye perspective is distorted such that straight lines appear curved. Sometimes, a fisheye attachment is called a **panoramic** attachment because software can convert a fisheye image into a panorama (a perspective-corrected image with a wide aspect ratio).

- **Macro** or **close-up** attachment: This enables the lens to focus at a short distance in order to capture a sharp image at a high level of magnification, comparable to a magnifying glass.

- **Microscope** attachment: This enables a more extreme level of magnification, comparable to a microscope. The focus distance is so short that the lens attachment may almost touch the subject. Typically, the attachment includes a ring of LED lights to illuminate the subject.

Typically, a lens attachment might cost between $20 and $50. The sharpness of the optics can vary greatly, so try to compare reviews before you choose a product. A fisheye attachment could be a fun accessory for our photographic work in *Chapter 2, Capturing, Storing, and Sharing Photos*. A macro, close-up, or microscope attachment could be useful for our work with small objects in *Chapter 5, Classifying Coins and Commodities*. Generally, you can experiment with any lens attachment in any chapter's project.

Summary

This chapter has introduced the software and hardware that we will use to make computer vision applications for iOS. We set up a development environment, including Xcode, the iOS SDK, the Xcode Command Line Tools, a prebuilt version of OpenCV's standard modules, and optionally a custom-built version of OpenCV's extra modules. Using these tools and libraries, we developed an iOS application that performs a basic image processing function and we built it for iOS simulators and local devices. We discussed some of the places where we can seek more information about Apple's app distribution process, the iOS SDK, and OpenCV. Finally, we compared the camera specifications of iOS devices and learned about accessories that may help us capture clearer and more specialized images. The next chapter delves deeper into the topics of computational photography and image processing as we will build an application that can capture, edit, and share photographs.

2
Capturing, Storing, and Sharing Photos

For many people, photography is a collaborative and social activity. This is not just a new perspective. Even the pioneers of photography spent long hours sharing their creative processes with family, students, models, and curious members of the public, who hoped to be immortalized in this new art form.

Today's technology enables people to collaborate and socialize in a short time and at a great distance. As we discussed in the previous chapter, the iPhone offers a set of unobtrusive and intuitive tools to any user who wants to capture, edit, and share photos from this small screen. For better or worse, a few taps of the user's fingers have replaced all the manual work of the studio, darkroom, print shop, and delivery service.

This chapter addresses the technical challenges of developing a mobile workflow for the social photographer. We will accomplish the following tasks:

- Configure the camera, including focus and exposure settings
- Process images from the camera
- Show a real-time preview that reflects the current scene, camera settings, and image processing settings
- Save an image to the user's Photos library
- Post an image and message to the user's followers on Facebook, Twitter, Sina Weibo, or Tencent Weibo
- Use various standard GUI features, including touch interactions, toolbar items, alerts, and composition dialogs

We will combine this functionality to make a basic photo sharing application. This app will also provide a foundation for our work in *Chapter 3*, *Blending Images*, where we will add more image processing options. As photography allows us to work with light as a medium, let's call our app LightWork.

 To obtain the completed projects for this book, you can refer to my GitHub repository at `https://github.com/JoeHowse/iOSWithOpenCV` or log in to your account on Packt Publishing's site at `https://www.packtpub.com/`. The project for *Chapter 2*, *Capturing, Storing, and Sharing Photos* and *Chapter 3*, *Blending Images*, is in the `LightWork` subfolder.

Planning a photo sharing application

When it opens, LightWork will present a vintage photograph and toolbar containing a few items. The following screenshot shows it all:

This bucolic image is an early color photograph, shot in 1902 by Adolf Miethe, a German photographer, professor, and inventor. The photo almost looks like a painting due to its coarse grain and pastel colors. However, it is a true example of a color photographic process. Miethe captured a scene on three photographic plates behind three different filters: red, green, and blue. Then, to recreate a multicolored image, he superimposed the three images using a projection process with different colors of light or a printing process with different dyes. Similar techniques are still in use today in our digital sensors, monitors, and printers.

LightWork will also be capable of displaying a live preview from a camera. However, for our purposes, a static (still) image is also a useful preview. A static image (unlike a camera preview) can be displayed in an iPhone simulator, so it enables us to test our code without a real device. Moreover, our chosen static image contains a variety of hues and brightness levels, so users may treat it as a standard, representative scene that helps them study image processing effects.

The leftmost item in the toolbar is a **segmented control** (a set of mutually exclusive buttons) with two options: **Color** and **Gray**. If **Color** is selected, the image will be displayed normally. If **Gray** is selected, the image will be displayed in grayscale. We will achieve the grayscale effect through a combination of camera settings and image processing.

Next, to the right of the segmented control, is a button with the standard switch camera icon. This button lets the user cycle through the static image, front camera, and rear camera. The first time the user taps the button, the static image will disappear and be replaced with a live preview of the front camera (the *selfie* camera). If the user taps the button a second time, the live preview will switch to the rear camera. The third time, the live preview will disappear and the static image will reappear, completing the cycle. The following screenshot shows the live preview of the rear camera.

Note that the app is designed to display the preview in a **letterboxed** mode, meaning that the top and bottom remain black so that the live video's aspect ratio is preserved:

Finally, at the center of the toolbar is a **Save** button. When the user taps it, LightWork will temporarily disable all toolbar items and display a spinning busy indicator. Meanwhile, the current image will be saved to the Photos library. Later, anytime the user opens the Photos app, the image will be visible there. LightWork will also display an alert to ask whether the user wants to share the photo via social media. Depending on the social media accounts that are set up on the device, the alert may offer as many as four sharing options: Facebook, Twitter, Sina Weibo, and Tencent Weibo. The following screenshot shows the alert that a user will see if only a Twitter account is set up on the device:

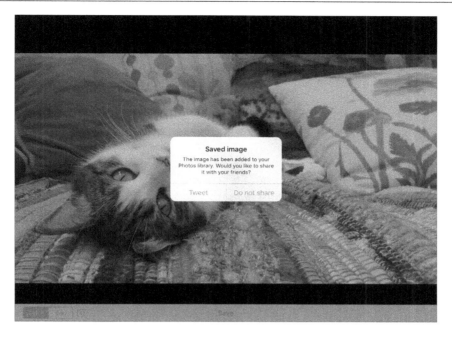

If the user opts to share the image, a standard message composition dialog will appear, as seen in the following screenshot:

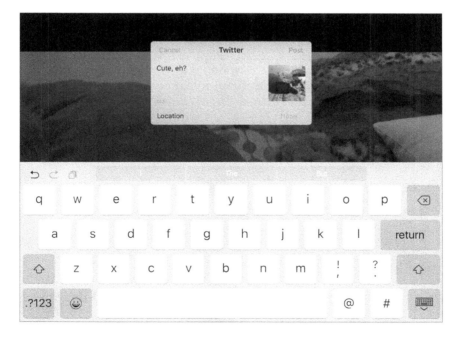

The user may type a message and post it along with the image. Alternatively, the user may cancel the composition. Either way, the composition dialog will disappear. LightWork will re-enable the toolbar items, so, once again, the user may configure the camera, select image processing effects, and capture new photos.

[I thank my cat, Josephine, for her participation in this social experiment.]

Our user interface will have one more feature. When the user taps the video, LightWork will configure the camera to focus on the tapped point. The exposure will also be adjusted so that the point is neither too bright nor too dark.

Configuring the project

Create an Xcode project named LightWork using the **Single View Application** template. Configure the project according to the instructions in the *Configuring the project* section in *Chapter 1, Setting Up Software and Hardware*. Next, we will take a few additional configuration steps because LightWork depends on more frameworks and requires a camera.

Adding frameworks

Besides its dependency on opencv2.framework, LightWork also depends on the following standard frameworks from the iOS SDK:

- Accelerate.framework: This is optional but recommended because it enables OpenCV to use advanced optimizations
- AssetsLibrary.framework
- AVFoundation.framework
- CoreGraphics.framework
- CoreMedia.framework
- CoreVideo.framework
- Photos.framework
- QuartzCore.framework
- Social.framework
- UIKit.framework

Add these frameworks to the **Build Phases | Link Binary With Libraries** section of the project settings.

Specifying the camera requirement

Currently, there is a camera in all devices that support iOS 9. However, perhaps in the future, some iOS devices will lack a camera. To cover this possibility and prevent the App Store from distributing our app to incompatible devices, we should explicitly specify that LightWork requires a camera.

Open `Info.plist`, expand the **Required device capabilities** item, add a new subitem, and enter the `video-camera` value. After you do this, the property list should look like the following screenshot:

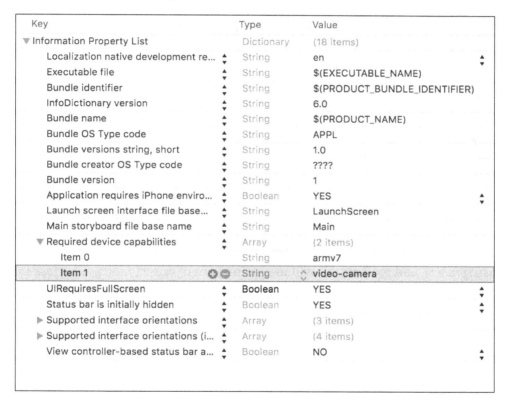

Key	Type	Value
▼ Information Property List	Dictionary	(18 items)
Localization native development re...	String	en
Executable file	String	$(EXECUTABLE_NAME)
Bundle identifier	String	$(PRODUCT_BUNDLE_IDENTIFIER)
InfoDictionary version	String	6.0
Bundle name	String	$(PRODUCT_NAME)
Bundle OS Type code	String	APPL
Bundle versions string, short	String	1.0
Bundle creator OS Type code	String	????
Bundle version	String	1
Application requires iPhone enviro...	Boolean	YES
Launch screen interface file base...	String	LaunchScreen
Main storyboard file base name	String	Main
▼ Required device capabilities	Array	(2 items)
Item 0	String	armv7
Item 1	String	video-camera
UIRequiresFullScreen	Boolean	YES
Status bar is initially hidden	Boolean	YES
▶ Supported interface orientations	Array	(3 items)
▶ Supported interface orientations (i...	Array	(4 items)
View controller-based status bar a...	Boolean	NO

For LightWork, we are specifying `video-camera` because we want to use a live video as a preview. If you have a project where you only care about capturing still images, you may specify `still-camera` instead.

Defining and laying out the view controller

As discussed in the previous chapter, we may declare GUI elements in a view controller's source code and lay them out in a storyboard. Thus, to begin, let's open `ViewController.m` and define the private interface of our `ViewController` class. The interface depends on headers from the iOS SDK's Photos and Social frameworks as well as the OpenCV framework. Moreover, it depends on headers that define the public interfaces of our own classes, `ViewController` and `VideoCamera`. The latter class will handle many aspects of camera input and video display and we will write it later in the *Controlling the camera* section. Let's import these dependencies by adding the following code at the start of `ViewController.m`:

```
#import <Photos/Photos.h>
#import <Social/Social.h>

#import <opencv2/core.hpp>
#import <opencv2/imgcodecs.hpp>
#import <opencv2/imgcodecs/ios.h>
#import <opencv2/imgproc.hpp>

#import "ViewController.h"
#import "VideoCamera.h"
```

Next, let's define the instance variables of the `ViewController` class. We will use several `cv::Mat` objects to store the static image and camera images in color or grayscale format. Our GUI objects will include an image view, activity indicator (a *busy spinner*), and toolbar. We will use an instance of our `VideoCamera` class to control the camera and grab and display video images. Finally, we will use a Boolean variable to keep track of whether the user pressed the **Save** button to save the upcoming frame. Here are the relevant variable declarations:

```
@interface ViewController () <CvVideoCameraDelegate> {
  cv::Mat originalStillMat;
  cv::Mat updatedStillMatGray;
  cv::Mat updatedStillMatRGBA;
  cv::Mat updatedVideoMatGray;
  cv::Mat updatedVideoMatRGBA;
}

@property IBOutlet UIImageView *imageView;
@property IBOutlet UIActivityIndicatorView *activityIndicatorView;
@property IBOutlet UIToolbar *toolbar;

@property VideoCamera *videoCamera;
@property BOOL saveNextFrame;
```

Note that the class name is followed by `<CvVideoCameraDelegate>`, meaning that the class implements a protocol named `CvVideoCameraDelegate`. This protocol is part of OpenCV and defines a method, `- (void)processImage:(cv::Mat &)mat`, for the handling of video frames. Later, in the *Controlling the camera* section, we will discuss how this callback method relates to our `VideoCamera` class.

 An Objective-C protocol is analogous to a C++ pure virtual class or a Java or C# interface. It declares methods but does not implement them.

Next, let's define methods of `VideoCamera`. Some of the methods are callbacks to handle a GUI event, such as a button being pressed. We must use the `IBAction` keyword to expose these methods to Interface Builder. Later in this section, when we edit the storyboard in Interface Builder, we will connect widgets to the `IBOutlet` properties and `IBAction` methods. Let's declare the following callbacks for the video preview's tap-to-focus feature, the **Color** or **Gray** segmented control, the switch camera button, and the **Save** button:

- `(IBAction)onTapToSetPointOfInterest:`
  `(UITapGestureRecognizer *)tapGesture;`
- `(IBAction)onColorModeSelected:`
  `(UISegmentedControl *)segmentedControl;`
- `(IBAction)onSwitchCameraButtonPressed;`
- `(IBAction)onSaveButtonPressed;`

Besides the `IBAction` callbacks, `VideoCamera` has several more methods. We will call a `refresh` method to update the display after a change in the camera's state or image processing settings. Other methods will facilitate processing, saving, and sharing images as well as starting and stopping the app's *busy* mode. Here are the relevant declarations:

- `(void)refresh;`
- `(void)processImage:(cv::Mat &)mat;`
- `(void)processImageHelper:(cv::Mat &)mat;`
- `(void)saveImage:(UIImage *)image;`
- `(void)showSaveImageFailureAlertWithMessage:(NSString *)message;`
- `(void)showSaveImageSuccessAlertWithImage:(UIImage *)image;`
- `(UIAlertAction *)shareImageActionWithTitle:(NSString *)title`
  `serviceType:(NSString *)serviceType image:(UIImage *)image;`
- `(void)startBusyMode;`
- `(void)stopBusyMode;`

`@end`

Now that we have completed the interface declarations in `ViewController.m`, let's open `Main.storyboard`. We need to lay out the following widgets:

- A `UIImageView` filling the background.
- A `UIActivityIndicatorView` in the center.
- A `UIToolbar` at the bottom. It should contain the following `UIBarButtonItem` widgets from left to right:
  - A custom toolbar item containing `UISegmentedControl`
  - A button with the standard switch camera icon
  - A flexible space
  - A button with the standard **Save** label
  - Another flexible space

Refer to the following screenshot as a layout guide (or just download the completed storyboard from the book's GitHub repository):

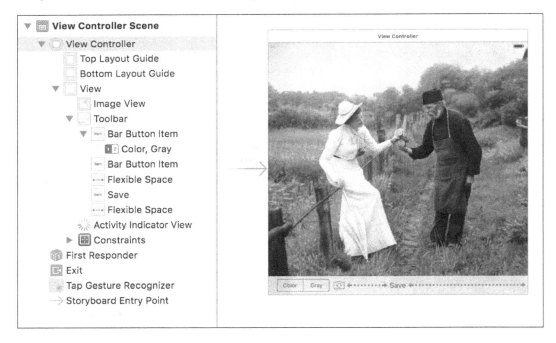

 Remember to apply constraints to the widgets so that the layout supports any screen resolution and aspect ratio.

After completing the layout, we must make the image view respond to touch interactions so that the user can tap to focus. Add a `UITapGestureRecognizer` by dragging a **Tap Gesture Recognizer** item from the library pane to the image view. Select **Image View** in the scene hierarchy and, in the inspector, ensure that **User Interaction Enabled** is checked.

Next, we must connect the widgets to the `IBOutlet` and `IBAction` hooks that we defined in `ViewController.m`. Right-click on **View Controller** in the scene hierarchy to see the list of available outlets and actions. Set the connections so that they match the following screenshot:

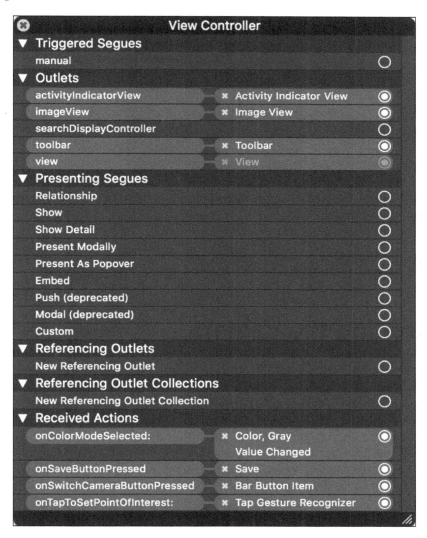

When we connect the `onColorModeSelected:` action to the **Color, Gray** segmented control, Interface Builder will present a menu of the events that the segmented control supports, as seen in the following screenshot:

Choose the **Value Changed** event, which occurs when the user selects a new option in the segmented control.

 Standard toolbar buttons support only a single event, so when we connect these items, Interface Builder does not present a menu of events.

Controlling the camera

The iOS SDK and OpenCV provide several programming interfaces for camera control. Within the iOS SDK, **AVFoundation** is the general-purpose framework for all recording and playback of **audiovisual (AV)** content. AVFoundation provides complete access to the iOS camera's parameters, including the image format, focus, exposure, flash, frame rate, and digital zoom (crop factor). However, AVFoundation does not solve any GUI problems. The application developer may create a custom camera GUI, use a higher-level framework that provides a GUI, or automate the camera so that it operates without GUI input. AVFoundation is sufficiently flexible to support any of these designs, but this flexibility comes at a price as AVFoundation is complex.

The official AVFoundation Programming Guide is located at `https://developer.apple.com/library/ios/documentation/AudioVideo/Conceptual/AVFoundationPG`.

The iOS SDK implements a standard camera GUI in the `UIImagePickerController` class, which builds atop AVFoundation. This GUI enables the user to configure the camera and capture a photo or video. The application developer may handle the photo or video after its capture, but the options to customize the controls and video preview are somewhat limited. Thus, `UIImagePickerController` is not ideal for our LightWork application, which will provide a custom preview of the processed images.

 For an official guide to `UIImagePickerController`, see Camera Programming Topics for iOS at `https://developer.apple.com/library/ios/documentation/AudioVideo/Conceptual/CameraAndPhotoLib_TopicsForIOS`.

OpenCV provides a class, `CvVideoCamera`, which implements high-level camera control functions and a preview GUI, but supports a high degree of customization. `CvVideoCamera` builds atop AVFoundation and offers access to some of the underlying classes. Thus, the application developer may opt to use a combination of high-level `CvVideoCamera` functionality and lower-level AVFoundation functionality. The application developer implements most of the GUI and may either disable the video preview or specify a parent view wherein `CvVideoCamera` will render it. Moreover, the application may handle each video frame as it is captured, and, if the application edits the captured frame in-place, `CvVideoCamera` will display the result in the preview. Thus, `CvVideoCamera` is an appropriate starting point for LightWork.

 OpenCV also provides a class called `CvPhotoCamera`, which is designed to capture high-quality still images instead of a continuous stream of video images. Unlike `CvVideoCamera`, `CvPhotoCamera` does not let us apply custom image processing to the live preview.

Subclassing CvVideoCamera

CvVideoCamera is an Objective-C class, and Objective-C lets us override *any* instance method or property in a subclass. Moreover, as OpenCV is open source, we can study CvVideoCamera's entire implementation. Thus, we have the power and knowledge to make a subclass that reimplements pieces of CvVideoCamera with modifications. This is a convenient way to tweak or patch an open source class's implementation without modifying and rebuilding the library's source code.

 You can view CvVideoCamera's latest implementation in OpenCV's GitHub repository at https://github.com/Itseez/opencv/blob/master/modules/videoio/src/cap_ios_video_camera.mm.

Currently, in OpenCV 3.1, CvVideoCamera has significant bugs, including the following:

- Depending on the requested quality settings, the resolution may default to an incorrect value
- Depending on the device orientation, the preview and captured image may be rotated incorrectly, and the preview may be stretched to an incorrect aspect ratio

We will create a subclass called VideoCamera in order to patch these issues and provide extra functionality. Add a new header file called VideoCamera.h. Here, we will declare the subclass's public interface, including a new property and method, as seen in the following code:

```
#import <opencv2/videoio/cap_ios.h>

@interface VideoCamera : CvVideoCamera

@property BOOL letterboxPreview;

- (void)setPointOfInterestInParentViewSpace:(CGPoint)point;

@end
```

When the letterboxPreview property is YES, VideoCamera will display the video preview in a letterboxed mode. Otherwise, the preview may appear in a cropped mode, which is equivalent to the superclass's behavior.

The set PointOfInterestInParentViewSpace: method will set a point of interest for the camera's autofocus and autoexposure algorithms. After a brief search for an optimal solution, the camera should reconfigure itself so that its focal distance and midtone level match the neighborhood of the given point, which is expressed in pixel coordinates within the preview's parent view. In other words, after the adjustment, the point and its neighborhood should be in focus and approximately as bright as 50% gray. However, a good autoexposure algorithm may allow variances in brightness depending on the color and the scene's other regions.

[The autofocus and autoexposure algorithms are not specified in the iOS SDK documentation. They may be device-specific.]

Now, let's create the class's implementation file, VideoCamera.m. We will add a private interface with a property, customPreviewLayer, as seen in the following code:

```
#import "VideoCamera.h"

@interface VideoCamera ()

@property (nonatomic, retain) CALayer *customPreviewLayer;

@end
```

We will implement customPreviewLayer so that it accesses a variable, _customPreviewLayer, which is defined in the superclass's private interface. This variable is the video preview layer and we will customize its position and size in VideoCamera. Here is the code that begins implementation of VideoCamera and sets up the relationship between the property and variable:

```
@implementation VideoCamera

@synthesize customPreviewLayer = _customPreviewLayer;
```

To customize the layout of the preview layer, we will override the following methods of CvVideoCamera:

- (int)imageWidth and (int)imageHeight: These getters should return the horizontal and vertical resolution that the camera is currently using. The superclass's implementation is buggy (in OpenCV 3.1) because it relies on a set of assumptions about the default resolution in various quality modes instead of directly querying the current resolution.

- (void) updateSize: The superclass uses this method to make its assumptions about the camera's resolution. This is actually a counterproductive method. As described in the previous bullet point, the assumptions are unreliable and unnecessary.

- (void) layoutPreviewLayer: This method should lay out the preview in a manner that respects the current device orientation. The superclass's implementation is buggy (in OpenCV 3.1). The preview is stretched or incorrectly oriented in some cases.

To get the correct resolution, we can query the camera's current capture parameters via an AVFoundation class called AVCaptureVideoDataOutput. Refer to the following code, which overrides the imageWidth getter:

```
- (int)imageWidth {
  AVCaptureVideoDataOutput *output =
    [self.captureSession.outputs lastObject];
  NSDictionary *videoSettings = [output videoSettings];
  int videoWidth =
    [[videoSettings objectForKey:@"Width"] intValue];
  return videoWidth;
}
```

Similarly, let's override the imageHeight getter in the following code:

```
- (int)imageHeight {
  AVCaptureVideoDataOutput *output =
    [self.captureSession.outputs lastObject];
  NSDictionary *videoSettings = [output videoSettings];
  int videoHeight =
    [[videoSettings objectForKey:@"Height"] intValue];
  return videoHeight;
}
```

 Our implementations of imageWidth and imageHeight will return 0 if the camera is not currently running. For LightWork's purposes, this behavior does not cause any problems.

At this point, we have adequately solved the problem of querying the camera resolution. Thus, we can override the updateSize method with an empty implementation:

```
- (void)updateSize {
  // Do nothing.
}
```

When laying out the video preview, first we center it within the parent view. Then, we find its aspect ratio and choose a preview size that respects the aspect ratio. If letterboxPreview is YES, the preview may be smaller than its parent view in one of the dimensions. Otherwise, it may be larger than its parent view in one of the dimensions, and, in this case, its extremities may be offscreen and therefore cropped. The following code shows how we position and size the preview:

```
- (void)layoutPreviewLayer {
  if (self.parentView != nil) {

    // Center the video preview.
    self.customPreviewLayer.position = CGPointMake(
      0.5 * self.parentView.frame.size.width,
      0.5 * self.parentView.frame.size.height);

    // Find the video's aspect ratio.
    CGFloat videoAspectRatio = self.imageWidth /
      (CGFloat)self.imageHeight;

    // Scale the video preview while maintaining its aspect ratio.
    CGFloat boundsW;
    CGFloat boundsH;
    if (self.imageHeight > self.imageWidth) {
      if (self.letterboxPreview) {
        boundsH = self.parentView.frame.size.height;
        boundsW = boundsH * videoAspectRatio;
      } else {
        boundsW = self.parentView.frame.size.width;
        boundsH = boundsW / videoAspectRatio;
      }
    } else {
      if (self.letterboxPreview) {
        boundsW = self.parentView.frame.size.width;
        boundsH = boundsW / videoAspectRatio;
      } else {
        boundsH = self.parentView.frame.size.height;
        boundsW = boundsH * videoAspectRatio;
      }
    }
    self.customPreviewLayer.bounds = CGRectMake(
      0.0, 0.0, boundsW, boundsH);
  }
}
```

Next, let's consider the `setPointOfInterestInParentViewSpace:` method. Its implementation will involve several cases, yet the concept is rather simple. As an argument, we accept a point in the coordinate system of the preview's parent view. This is a convenient coordinate system if we assume that the caller is a view controller. AVFoundation lets us specify a point of interest for focus and exposure, but it uses a proportional landscape-right coordinate system. This means that the upper-left corner is (0.0, 0.0), the lower-right corner is (1.0, 1.0), and the axis directions are based on the landscape-right orientation regardless of the device's actual orientation. **Landscape-right** orientation means that the device's home button is on the user's right-hand side. Thus, positive X points toward the home button and positive Y points away from the volume buttons. Here is our method's implementation, which checks the camera's autoexposure and autofocus capabilities, performs the coordinate conversion, validates the coordinates, and sets the point of interest via AVFoundation functionality:

```
- (void)setPointOfInterestInParentViewSpace:
    (CGPoint)parentViewPoint {

  if (!self.running) {
    return;
  }

  // Find the current capture device.
  NSArray *captureDevices =
    [AVCaptureDevice devicesWithMediaType:AVMediaTypeVideo];
  AVCaptureDevice *captureDevice;
  for (captureDevice in captureDevices) {
    if (captureDevice.position ==
        self.defaultAVCaptureDevicePosition) {
      break;
    }
  }

  BOOL canSetFocus = [captureDevice
      isFocusModeSupported:AVCaptureFocusModeAutoFocus] &&
    captureDevice.isFocusPointOfInterestSupported;

  BOOL canSetExposure = [captureDevice
      isExposureModeSupported:AVCaptureExposureModeAutoExpose] &&
    captureDevice.isExposurePointOfInterestSupported;

  if (!canSetFocus && !canSetExposure) {
```

```
    return;
  }

  if (![captureDevice lockForConfiguration:nil]) {
    return;
  }

  // Find the preview's offset relative to the parent view.
  CGFloat offsetX = 0.5 * (self.parentView.bounds.size.width -
    self.customPreviewLayer.bounds.size.width);
  CGFloat offsetY = 0.5 * (self.parentView.bounds.size.height -
    self.customPreviewLayer.bounds.size.height);

  // Find the focus coordinates, proportional to the preview size.
  CGFloat focusX = (parentViewPoint.x - offsetX) /
    self.customPreviewLayer.bounds.size.width;
  CGFloat focusY = (parentViewPoint.y - offsetY) /
    self.customPreviewLayer.bounds.size.height;

  if (focusX < 0.0 || focusX > 1.0 ||
      focusY < 0.0 || focusY > 1.0) {
    // The point is outside the preview.
    return;
  }

  // Adjust the focus coordinates based on the orientation.
  // They should be in the landscape-right coordinate system.
  switch (self.defaultAVCaptureVideoOrientation) {
    case AVCaptureVideoOrientationPortraitUpsideDown: {
      CGFloat oldFocusX = focusX;
      focusX = 1.0 - focusY;
      focusY = oldFocusX;
      break;
    }
    case AVCaptureVideoOrientationLandscapeLeft: {
      focusX = 1.0 - focusX;
      focusY = 1.0 - focusY;
      break;
    }
    case AVCaptureVideoOrientationLandscapeRight: {
      // Do nothing.
      break;
    }
```

```
      default: { // Portrait
        CGFloat oldFocusX = focusX;
        focusX = focusY;
        focusY = 1.0 - oldFocusX;
        break;
      }
  }

  if (self.defaultAVCaptureDevicePosition ==
      AVCaptureDevicePositionFront) {
    // De-mirror the X coordinate.
    focusX = 1.0 - focusX;
  }

  CGPoint focusPoint = CGPointMake(focusX, focusY);

  if (canSetFocus) {
    // Auto-focus on the selected point.
    captureDevice.focusMode = AVCaptureFocusModeAutoFocus;
    captureDevice.focusPointOfInterest = focusPoint;
  }

  if (canSetExposure) {
    // Auto-expose for the selected point.
    captureDevice.exposureMode = AVCaptureExposureModeAutoExpose;
    captureDevice.exposurePointOfInterest = focusPoint;
  }

  [captureDevice unlockForConfiguration];
}

@end
```

At this point, we have implemented a class that is capable of configuring a camera and capturing frames. However, we still need to implement another class to choose a configuration and receive the frames.

Using the CvVideoCamera subclass in the view controller

Open `ViewController.m` and review our declaration of `ViewController`'s private interface. Our class implements the `CvVideoCameraDelegate` protocol and has a `VideoCamera` as a property. It also has a copy of the static image that we will use as a placeholder when the camera is not active. As usual, we will initialize things in the view controller's `viewDidLoad` method. First, we will load the static image from file and convert it to an appropriate format. Then, we will create the instance of `VideoCamera` with our image view as the preview's parent view. We will tell the camera to send its frames to this view controller (`delegate`) and to use a high-resolution mode at 30 FPS, with a letterboxed preview. Here is the implementation of `viewDidLoad`:

```
- (void)viewDidLoad {
  [super viewDidLoad];

  UIImage *originalStillImage = [UIImage imageNamed:@"Fleur.jpg"];
  UIImageToMat(originalStillImage, originalStillMat);

  self.videoCamera =
    [[VideoCamera alloc] initWithParentView:self.imageView];
  self.videoCamera.delegate = self;
  self.videoCamera.defaultAVCaptureSessionPreset =
    AVCaptureSessionPresetHigh;
  self.videoCamera.defaultFPS = 30;
  self.videoCamera.letterboxPreview = YES;
}
```

> For iPhone 6 and 6 Plus, the rear camera supports a maximum frame rate of 240 FPS at 1280x720 resolution. See the specifications in Apple's *Technical Note TN2409* at https://developer.apple.com/library/ios/technotes/tn2409/. A high frame rate will make the preview look smoother and more responsive and will facilitate the capture of fast-moving objects. However, it will also impose a greater burden on the device's processors and drain the battery faster.

We will also override another UIViewController method called viewDidLayoutSubviews. This runs after viewDidLoad and after the view controller has assessed all aspects of the layout, including the orientation. Note that the method will be called again whenever the orientation changes. Here, we will configure the camera's orientation to match the device orientation, as seen in the following code:

```
- (void)viewDidLayoutSubviews {
  [super viewDidLayoutSubviews];

  switch ([UIDevice currentDevice].orientation) {
    case UIDeviceOrientationPortraitUpsideDown:
      self.videoCamera.defaultAVCaptureVideoOrientation =
        AVCaptureVideoOrientationPortraitUpsideDown;
      break;
    case UIDeviceOrientationLandscapeLeft:
      self.videoCamera.defaultAVCaptureVideoOrientation =
        AVCaptureVideoOrientationLandscapeLeft;
      break;
    case UIDeviceOrientationLandscapeRight:
      self.videoCamera.defaultAVCaptureVideoOrientation =
        AVCaptureVideoOrientationLandscapeRight;
      break;
    default:
      self.videoCamera.defaultAVCaptureVideoOrientation =
        AVCaptureVideoOrientationPortrait;
      break;
  }

  [self refresh];
}
```

Note that we call a helper method, refresh, after reconfiguring the camera. We will implement refresh later in this section. It will ensure that the camera is restarted or the static image is reprocessed to reflect the latest configuration.

When the user taps the preview's parent view, we will find the coordinates of the tap and pass them to the setPointOfInterestInParentViewSpace: method, which we implemented previously in VideoCamera. Here is the relevant callback for the tap event:

```
- (IBAction)onTapToSetPointOfInterest:
    (UITapGestureRecognizer *)tapGesture {
  if (tapGesture.state == UIGestureRecognizerStateEnded) {
    if (self.videoCamera.running) {
      CGPoint tapPoint =
```

```
      [tapGesture locationInView:self.imageView];
    [self.videoCamera
      setPointOfInterestInParentViewSpace:tapPoint];
  }
 }
}
```

When the user selects **Gray** or **Color** in the segmented control, we will set the
VideoCamera's grayscaleMode property to YES or NO. This property is inherited from
CvVideoCamera. After setting grayscaleMode, we will call our ViewController's refresh helper
method to restart the camera with the appropriate settings. Here is the callback to
handle the change in the segmented control's state:

```
- (IBAction)onColorModeSelected:
    (UISegmentedControl *)segmentedControl {
  switch (segmentedControl.selectedSegmentIndex) {
    case 0:
      self.videoCamera.grayscaleMode = NO;
      break;
    default:
      self.videoCamera.grayscaleMode = YES;
      break;
  }
  [self refresh];
}
```

When the user taps the switch camera button, we will activate the next camera or
cycle back to the static image of the lady and gardener. During each transition,
we must ensure that the previous camera is stopped or the previous static image
is hidden and the next camera is started or the next static image is processed and
displayed. Again, our refresh helper method is useful. Here is the implementation
of the button's callback:

```
- (IBAction)onSwitchCameraButtonPressed {

  if (self.videoCamera.running) {
    switch (self.videoCamera.defaultAVCaptureDevicePosition) {
      case AVCaptureDevicePositionFront:
        self.videoCamera.defaultAVCaptureDevicePosition =
          AVCaptureDevicePositionBack;
        [self refresh];
        break;
      default:
        [self.videoCamera stop];
```

```
            [self refresh];
            break;
        }
    }

    else {
      // Hide the still image.
      self.imageView.image = nil;

      self.videoCamera.defaultAVCaptureDevicePosition =
        AVCaptureDevicePositionFront;
      [self.videoCamera start];
    }
}
```

The refresh helper method will check whether a camera is running. If yes, we will ensure that the static image is hidden and we will stop and restart the camera. Otherwise (if no camera is running), we will reprocess the static image and display the result. The processing consists of converting the image to an appropriate color format and passing it to the processImage: method. Remember that CvVideoCamera and our VideoCamera subclass likewise pass video frames to the processImage: method of a CvVideoCameraDelegate, such as our ViewController class. Here, in refresh, we are reusing the same image processing method for the static image instead. Let's look at the refresh method's implementation:

```
- (void)refresh {

    if (self.videoCamera.running) {
      // Hide the still image.
      self.imageView.image = nil;

      // Restart the video.
      [self.videoCamera stop];
      [self.videoCamera start];
    }

    else {
      // Refresh the still image.
      UIImage *image;
      if (self.videoCamera.grayscaleMode) {
        cv::cvtColor(originalStillMat, updatedStillMatGray,
          cv::COLOR_RGBA2GRAY);
        [self processImage:updatedStillMatGray];
```

```
      image = MatToUIImage(updatedStillMatGray);
    } else {
      cv::cvtColor(originalStillMat, updatedStillMatRGBA,
        cv::COLOR_RGBA2BGRA);
      [self processImage:updatedStillMatRGBA];
      cv::cvtColor(updatedStillMatRGBA, updatedStillMatRGBA,
        cv::COLOR_BGRA2RGBA);
      image = MatToUIImage(updatedStillMatRGBA);
    }
    self.imageView.image = image;
  }
}
```

The `processImage:` method will have several responsibilities. First, it will correct another library bug. `CvVideoCamera` (in OpenCV 3.1) captures the image upside down when it is in landscape mode. This is easier to correct in postprocessing (in `processImage:`), rather than in our `VideoCamera` subclass. After ensuring that the image's rotation is correct, we will pass it to another method called `processImageHelper:`, which will be a convenient place to implement the majority of our image processing functionality. Finally, if the user has recently clicked on the **Save** button, we will convert the image to an appropriate format and pass it to a `saveImage:` helper method. Here is the relevant code:

```
- (void)processImage:(cv::Mat &)mat {

  if (self.videoCamera.running) {
    switch (self.videoCamera.defaultAVCaptureVideoOrientation) {
      case AVCaptureVideoOrientationLandscapeLeft:
      case AVCaptureVideoOrientationLandscapeRight:
        // The landscape video is captured upside-down.
        // Rotate it by 180 degrees.
        cv::flip(mat, mat, -1);
        break;
      default:
        break;
    }
  }

  [self processImageHelper:mat];

  if (self.saveNextFrame) {
    // The video frame, 'mat', is not safe for long-running
    // operations such as saving to file. Thus, we copy its
    // data to another cv::Mat first.
```

```
      UIImage *image;
      if (self.videoCamera.grayscaleMode) {
        mat.copyTo(updatedVideoMatGray);
        image = MatToUIImage(updatedVideoMatGray);
      } else {
        cv::cvtColor(mat, updatedVideoMatRGBA, cv::COLOR_BGRA2RGBA);
        image = MatToUIImage(updatedVideoMatRGBA);
      }
      [self saveImage:image];
      self.saveNextFrame = NO;
    }
  }
```

So far, we have not done much image processing, just some color conversions and rotations. Let's add the following stub method, where we will perform additional image processing in *Chapter 3*, *Blending Images*:

```
- (void)processImageHelper:(cv::Mat &)mat {
  // TODO: Implement in Chapter 3.
}
```

Our `ViewController` class still needs to implement the `saveImage:` helper method as well as GUI functionality related to saving and sharing images. However, we have finished implementing the camera control functionality and provided a skeleton of an image processing chain, which starts and ends with some necessary color conversions.

Working with various color formats

As we have seen, OpenCV and the iOS SDK work with various formats for color and grayscale images and sometimes we need to convert between formats. Let's step back from the code for a few moments to discuss the differences between formats and the problems that can arise if we do not perform the correct conversions.

RGB, BGR, RGBA, and BGRA

You probably learned the 24-bit RGB color format long ago, the first time you picked a custom color in a paint program or word processor. A pixel's color is represented by a sequence of three values, each with a range of 0 to 255 (that is, 8 bits or 1 byte). The first value is the color's red component or **channel**, followed by green, and lastly blue. For example, the color of an amber traffic light is (255, 126, 0), a mixture of lots of red and some green, but no blue. A series of pixel data makes an image.

The 24-bit BGR format simply reverses the channel order. For example, the color of the amber traffic light is (0, 126, 255) in BGR format.

 Using RGB or BGR, 24 **bits per pixel** (**bpp**) is enough to represent subtle gradations of color. Typical screens and consumer video cameras are limited to 24 bpp. However, some high-end cameras and screens support 30 bpp or even more. For our projects on iOS, 24 bpp is a reasonable limit.

RGBA and BGRA add a fourth channel, **alpha**, which comes last in both formats. Alpha represents transparency, where 0 is fully transparent and 255 is fully opaque (assuming 8 bits per channel or 32 bits in total). Of course, "transparent" is not a wavelength of light, and an ordinary photo camera does not record any data to distinguish between reflected light (which bounces off an opaque surface) and transmitted light (which passes through a transparent material). Thus, an unprocessed photo may be considered opaque and, if it includes an alpha channel, the alpha values will all be 255. Transparency or alpha becomes a more meaningful concept if we want to blend portions of images selectively.

Generally, OpenCV uses 24-bit BGR or 32-bit BGRA for color images. `CvVideoCamera` captures images in the BGRA format. However, the iOS SDK generally uses the RGBA format, so we must remember to perform conversions or else the red and blue channels will be misinterpreted.

Let's visualize the effect of swapping the red and blue channels in a colorful image. On the left, we see Miethe's charming rural scene, wherein the elderly gardener gives the young lady a rose. On the right, we see a different fantasy, wherein Papa Smurf gives a blue cupcake to Goldie:

In this book's print version, all images appear in grayscale. To see them in color, download them from Packt Publishing's website at `https://www.packtpub.com/sites/default/files/downloads/iOSApplicationDevelopmentwithOpenCV3_ColorImages.pdf` or read the eBook.

If we write a program that mistakenly treats RGB images as BGR (or vice versa), we will see strange results like the right-hand image!

YUV and grayscale

Suppose that we want to use fewer than 24 bpp so that our images use less memory and can be processed in less time. To this end, we must sacrifice some of the subtle gradations of *color* that 24 bpp can represent in RGB or BGR. However, perhaps we want retain the ability to represent subtle gradations of *brightness*. Here, we encounter a key limitation of RGB and BGR. The brightness depends on *all three* channels, and when we sacrifice bits in *any* channel, we lose gradations of brightness!

The YUV color model solves this problem. The Y channel just represents brightness. The U channel represents blueness (versus greenness), while the V channel represents redness (also versus greenness). Some variants of YUV are **planar** formats, meaning that all the Y data are consecutive in memory, followed by all the U and V data. Other variants of YUV are **packed** formats, meaning that Y, U, and V data are interleaved, like R, G, and B data in RGB or BGR.

An example of a planar format is I420, which has 12 bpp. This includes an 8-bit Y value for every pixel in the full-resolution image as well as 4-bit U and 4-bit V values sampled at half the resolution.

An example of a packed format is YUYV, which has 16 bpp. This includes an 8-bit Y value for every pixel in the full-resolution image as well as 8-bit U and 8-bit V values sampled at half the resolution. Note that all these values are byte-sized. Each Y byte is interleaved with a U or V byte alternately, as the name YUYV suggests.

 An 8-bit Y channel captures the same gradations of brightness as the three channels of a 24-bit RGB or BGR image.

Again, in certain circumstances, we must perform conversions or else the channel data will be misinterpreted. The left-hand side image shows how an I420 planar image might look if we tried to interpret its data as grayscale. The right-hand side image shows how a YUVY packed image might look if we tried to interpret its data as RGB:

Note that sky and the lady's dress have high Y values. These become misinterpreted as high R values in the right-hand side image.

A grayscale image is equivalent to the Y plane of a planar YUV image. Typically, a video camera's firmware, or at least its drivers, can efficiently convert the captured video to a planar YUV format. Then, if an application just needs grayscale data, it can read or copy the Y plane. This approach is more efficient than the alternative of capturing RGB frames and converting them to grayscale. Thus, when a CvVideoCamera's grayscaleMode property is YES, it grabs a planar YUV frame and passes a copy of the Y plane to the processImage: method of CvVideoCameraDelegate.

Starting and stopping the busy mode

Remember that we want to show an activity indicator and disable all the toolbar items while LightWork is busy saving or sharing a photo. Conversely, when LightWork is no longer busy with the photo, we want to hide the activity indicator and re-enable the toolbar items. As these actions affect the GUI, we must ensure that they run on the app's main thread.

 If our code is running on a background thread, nothing will happen when we try to show or hide the activity indicator.

To run code on a specific thread, we can make a post to the thread's event queue. The iOS SDK provides a C function, dispatch_async, which takes a target queue and code block as arguments. Another C function, dispatch_get_main_queue(), enables us to get the main thread's event queue. Let's use these functions in the following helper method, which starts the busy mode:

```
- (void)startBusyMode {
  dispatch_async(dispatch_get_main_queue(), ^{
    [self.activityIndicatorView startAnimating];
    for (UIBarItem *item in self.toolbar.items) {
      item.enabled = NO;
    }
  });
}
```

Similarly, the following helper method serves to stop the busy mode:

```
- (void)stopBusyMode {
  dispatch_async(dispatch_get_main_queue(), ^{
    [self.activityIndicatorView stopAnimating];
    for (UIBarItem *item in self.toolbar.items) {
      item.enabled = YES;
    }
  });
}
```

Saving an image to the Photos library

When the user presses the **Save** button, we start the busy mode. Then, if the video camera is running, we prepare to save the next frame. Otherwise, we immediately save the processed version of the static image. Here is the event handler:

```
- (IBAction)onSaveButtonPressed {
  [self startBusyMode];
  if (self.videoCamera.running) {
    self.saveNextFrame = YES;
  } else {
    [self saveImage:self.imageView.image];
  }
}
```

A helper method, `saveImage:`, is responsible for the transactions with the filesystem and Photos library. First, we try to write a PNG file to the application's temporary directory. Then, we try to create an asset in the Photos library based on this file. As part of this process, the file is automatically copied. We call other helper methods to show an alert dialog, which will describe the success or failure of the transaction. Here is the method's implementation:

```
- (void)saveImage:(UIImage *)image {

  // Try to save the image to a temporary file.
  NSString *outputPath = [NSString stringWithFormat:@"%@%@",
    NSTemporaryDirectory(), @"output.png"];
  if (![UIImagePNGRepresentation(image) writeToFile:outputPath
      atomically:YES]) {

    // Show an alert describing the failure.
    [self showSaveImageFailureAlertWithMessage:@"The image could not
be saved to the temporary directory."];

    return;
  }

  // Try to add the image to the Photos library.
  NSURL *outputURL = [NSURL URLWithString:outputPath];
  PHPhotoLibrary *photoLibrary =
    [PHPhotoLibrary sharedPhotoLibrary];
  [photoLibrary performChanges:^{
    [PHAssetChangeRequest
      creationRequestForAssetFromImageAtFileURL:outputURL];
```

```
    } completionHandler:^(BOOL success, NSError *error) {
      if (success) {
        // Show an alert describing the success, with sharing
        // options.
        [self showSaveImageSuccessAlertWithImage:image];
      } else {
        // Show an alert describing the failure.
        [self showSaveImageFailureAlertWithMessage:
          error.localizedDescription];
      }
    }];
}
```

Displaying an alert

To build a typical alert, we need a title, a message, and one or more action buttons.
Each action button has a block of code that runs when the user presses the button.

As an example, let's study a helper method that displays an error popup with an **OK**
button. When the user presses the **OK** button, the alert will be dismissed and the app
will stop its busy mode. Here is the implementation:

```
- (void)showSaveImageFailureAlertWithMessage:(NSString *)message {
  UIAlertController* alert = [UIAlertController
    alertControllerWithTitle:@"Failed to save image"
    message:message preferredStyle:UIAlertControllerStyleAlert];
  UIAlertAction* okAction = [UIAlertAction actionWithTitle:@"OK"
    style:UIAlertActionStyleDefault
    handler:^(UIAlertAction * _Nonnull action) {
      [self stopBusyMode];
    }];
  [alert addAction:okAction];
  [self presentViewController:alert animated:YES completion:nil];
}
```

Sharing an image via social media

If LightWork successfully saved the image to the Photos library, we want to show the user another alert with sharing options. The following method checks the availability of various social media platforms and builds an alert with an action button for each available platform. Despite targeting different social media platforms, the action buttons are similar to each other, so we build them in a helper method, `shareImageActionWithTitle:serviceType:image:`. We also provide a **Do not share** action button that does nothing except stop the app's busy mode:

```objc
- (void)showSaveImageSuccessAlertWithImage:(UIImage *)image {

    // Create a "Saved image" alert.
    UIAlertController* alert = [UIAlertController
      alertControllerWithTitle:@"Saved image"
      message:@"The image has been added to your Photos library.
      Would you like to share it with your friends?"
      preferredStyle:UIAlertControllerStyleAlert];

    // If the user has a Facebook account on this device, add a
    // "Post on Facebook" button to the alert.
    if ([SLComposeViewController
        isAvailableForServiceType:SLServiceTypeFacebook]) {
      UIAlertAction* facebookAction = [self
        shareImageActionWithTitle:@"Post on Facebook"
        serviceType:SLServiceTypeFacebook image:image];
      [alert addAction:facebookAction];
    }

    // If the user has a Twitter account on this device, add a
    // "Tweet" button to the alert.
    if ([SLComposeViewController
        isAvailableForServiceType:SLServiceTypeTwitter]) {
      UIAlertAction* twitterAction = [self
        shareImageActionWithTitle:@"Tweet"
        serviceType:SLServiceTypeTwitter image:image];
      [alert addAction:twitterAction];
    }

    // If the user has a Sina Weibo account on this device, add a
    // "Post on Sina Weibo" button to the alert.
    if ([SLComposeViewController
        isAvailableForServiceType:SLServiceTypeSinaWeibo]) {
      UIAlertAction* sinaWeiboAction = [self
```

```
      shareImageActionWithTitle:@"Post on Sina Weibo"
      serviceType:SLServiceTypeSinaWeibo image:image];
    [alert addAction:sinaWeiboAction];
  }

  // If the user has a Tencent Weibo account on this device, add a
  // "Post on Tencent Weibo" button to the alert.
  if ([SLComposeViewController
      isAvailableForServiceType:SLServiceTypeTencentWeibo]) {
    UIAlertAction* tencentWeiboAction = [self
      shareImageActionWithTitle:@"Post on Tencent Weibo"
      serviceType:SLServiceTypeTencentWeibo image:image];
    [alert addAction:tencentWeiboAction];
  }

  // Add a "Do not share" button to the alert.
  UIAlertAction* doNotShareAction = [UIAlertAction
    actionWithTitle:@"Do not share"
    style:UIAlertActionStyleDefault
    handler:^(UIAlertAction * _Nonnull action) {
      [self stopBusyMode];
    }];
  [alert addAction:doNotShareAction];

  // Show the alert.
  [self presentViewController:alert animated:YES completion:nil];
}
```

When the user presses a sharing action button, we present a standard iOS composition dialog that targets the specified social media platform. We also attach the image to this composition. When the user cancels or sends the composition, we ensure that LightWork stops its busy mode. Here is the relevant helper method to build this type of action button:

```
- (UIAlertAction *)shareImageActionWithTitle:(NSString *)title
    serviceType:(NSString *)serviceType image:(UIImage *)image {
  UIAlertAction* action = [UIAlertAction actionWithTitle:title
    style:UIAlertActionStyleDefault
    handler:^(UIAlertAction * _Nonnull action) {
      SLComposeViewController *composeViewController =
        [SLComposeViewController
          composeViewControllerForServiceType:serviceType];
      [composeViewController addImage:image];
      [self presentViewController:composeViewController
```

```
      animated:YES completion:^{
        [self stopBusyMode];
      }];
  return action;
}
```

Running the application

At runtime, LightWork will prompt the user once for permission to access the camera and again for permission to access the Photos library. If the user refuses, the app will not function fully. However, the user may grant (or revoke) these permissions later in the **LightWork** section of the Settings application.

Summary

Already, in the LightWork app, we have implemented a custom workflow for mobile photographers. Particularly, we have focused on enabling the user to configure the camera, select image processing effects, see a preview in real time, and share an image via social media. However, we can still do more. We will devote the next chapter to the goal of expanding LightWork's repertoire of image processing effects. At the same time, we will explore the concepts of multiple exposure, image comparisons, and augmented reality. LightWork will become more than a photography app; it will also help us visualize the relationship between two scenes and thus deepen our appreciation of computer vision.

3
Blending Images

Let's complete our work on the LightWork app, which we started in *Chapter 2, Capturing, Storing, and Sharing Photos*. LightWork can already control the iOS device's cameras, capture an image, convert its format, save it, and share it via social media. However, the app is missing the ability to load and reprocess old images. We are going to change this by enabling the user to achieve the following results:

- Select an image from the user's Photos library.
- Select an algorithm that defines how to blend two images. We will support some simple arithmetic algorithms as well as an edge-finding algorithm that reduces one of the images to a line drawing.
- Using the selected blending algorithm, blend the selected image with the background. The background may be the LightWork app's static background image or a frame of live video from the camera.

Compared to the groundwork that we have already done, these additional features are simple, so this chapter is shorter. However, we are taking an important step toward more advanced projects. Most tasks in computer vision rely on the accumulation and comparison of data from multiple images. Blending photos is a fun way to begin to visualize this process and by the end of this chapter, we will see how even simple blending algorithms can help a user with practical problems.

 To obtain the completed projects for this book, you can refer to my GitHub repository at https://github.com/JoeHowse/iOSWithOpenCV or log in to your account on Packt Publishing's site at https://www.packtpub.com/. The project for *Chapter 2, Capturing, Storing, and Sharing Photos*, and *Chapter 3, Blending Images*, is in the LightWork subfolder.

Thinking about hybrid images

A photograph records the light in a particular slice of time and space. Often, in modern photography, the film or digital sensor is exposed for just a few milliseconds, and people perceive this time as a single moment. We, as viewers, may sometimes feel that a photograph is a testament, a tangible *moment of truth*, in which the facts and elements of a complex case are laid bare.

Consider the following photograph, taken by Kanu Gandhi in February 1940. Between 1938 and 1948, the photographer documented the private life of his great-uncle, Mahatma Gandhi, the Indian independence leader and pacifist philosopher. Here, we see the Mahatma (left) meditating with Rabindranath Tagore (right), the Nobel Prize-winning poet:

At first glance, we may interpret this as a documentary photo, which appeals to our curiosity about a private meeting between two famous men. We may imagine that we are simply studying the facts about the men's pose, their expressions, and their surroundings as we try to guess their thoughts. Now, look carefully at the bottom of the picture. Do you see that the two men are seated *above* a canopy of trees and the hem of Tagore's robe is fading away like a ghost?

The image is a partial double exposure. Between two exposures, the roll of film did not advance as far as it normally should. This is a common mechanical glitch and causes a section of film to be exposed twice, producing a ghostly double-image. The double exposure is probably accidental in this case, but we can imagine that Kanu Gandhi was pleased with the result.

Again, look at the whole image and consider how the partial double exposure contributes to your impressions. Although the two men are looking down, we may imagine that they are aware of the trees and sky above them. The image conveys the sense that the canopy is vast and all around. This sense of openness is especially unusual in a square photo with a close and low vantage point. The rendition of the scene has, quite literally, broken a boundary between two times and places and gives us a perspective that is both intimate and grand.

With a film camera and darkroom, the creation of hybrid images is slow and thoughtful work. The photographer must have foresight and perseverance and keep an open mind about accidental results. Starting in the 1990s, scanners and image editing software began to enable a broader audience to create hybrid images. When I was 12, my father and I took a course in Photoshop and I was impressed by the software's fundamental concept that an image is a mixture of layers. I learned how to scan photographs, lay them atop each other, make parts of them transparent, and select an algorithm or blending mode to mix the opaque parts. With a 33 MHz CPU, this process was not exactly fast, but compared to anything I could do by hand, I thought it was amazing!

Today, Photoshop is fast on most hardware, and there are excellent free alternatives such as the **GNU Image Manipulation Program** (**GIMP**). Moreover, if we use a digital camera, we do not need a scanner! We can quickly build a library of photos and experiment with ways of blending them.

GIMP's documentation describes its blending modes at `https://docs.gimp.org/en/gimp-concepts-layer-modes.html` with formulae and examples. Photoshop's documentation describes its blending modes at `https://helpx.adobe.com/photoshop/using/blending-modes.html` with examples but not formulae. With OpenCV, these blending modes can be implemented as combinations of arithmetic functions such as `cv::addWeighted`, `cv::subtract`, and `cv::multiply`, which are described in the API documentation at `http://docs.opencv.org/3.1.0/d2/de8/group__core__array.html`.

The default blending mode in Photoshop and GIMP is a weighted average of the upper layer and lower layer. Another blending mode, called **Screen**, resembles double exposure. Assuming that we are working with 8 bits (256 levels) per color channel, **Screen** applies the following formula to each channel of each pixel:

```
dst = (255 - (255 - scrUpper) * (255 - srcLower)) / 255
```

This mode tends to produce a blend that is bright, like a double exposure. Conversely, a mode called **Multiply** tends to produce a dark blend, using the following formula:

```
dst = srcUpper * srcLower / 255
```

We will implement **Screen**, **Multiply**, and a simple **Average** blending mode in LightWork. We will also implement an original blending mode, which we will call **HUD** because it will resemble a heads-up display (HUD). A HUD is a transparent screen of the kind used in airplane cockpits. Here is a photo of a HUD in an F/A-18C Hornet jet:

If you are viewing the e-book, you will see that the HUD's text and lines have a yellowish green color, which is commonly used in HUDs because this color stands out against most backgrounds. Our **HUD** blending mode will find text and other sharp lines in the upper layer, tint them yellowish-green, and then superimpose them on the lower layer using the same formula as **Screen**.

To find sharp edges, we will rely on a type of algorithm called a **kernel filter** or **convolution matrix**. Each pixel in the output image is a weighted average of a neighborhood of pixels in the input image. Depending on the weights, a kernel filter may achieve various effects. It may blur an image, sharpen it, or even reduce it to a high-contrast representation of edge and non-edge regions. Consider the following examples of kernel weights for a 3 x 3 input neighborhood:

Blur		
1/9	1/9	1/9
1/9	1/9	1/9
1/9	1/9	1/9

Sharpen		
0	-1	0
-1	5	-1
0	-1	0

Find edges (Laplacian)		
0	1	0
1	-4	1
0	1	0

Photoshop, GIMP, and OpenCV implement a generalized kernel filter and a large variety of special cases, including the **Gaussian blur** effect and **Laplacian** edge-finding effect. Our **HUD** blending mode will apply a Gaussian blur filter to reduce noise and then a Laplacian filter to find edges.

GIMP's documentation describes convolution matrices at `https://docs.gimp.org/en/plug-in-convmatrix.html`, and Photoshop's documentation describes them at `https://helpx.adobe.com/photoshop/using/filter-effects-reference.html`. Photoshop's generalized implementation is called the "Custom" filter. OpenCV's generalized implementation is the `cv::filter2d` function, while specialized implementations include `cv::GaussianBlur` and `cv::Laplacian`. See the API documentation at `http://docs.opencv.org/3.1.0/d4/d86/group__imgproc__filter.html`.

The ability to selectively blend two images in real time is a step toward **augmented reality (AR)**. AR includes a broad range of technologies that enable a user to perceive a virtual environment as if it were part of the real environment. For example, consider the following screenshot from a drone navigation application used by NASA:

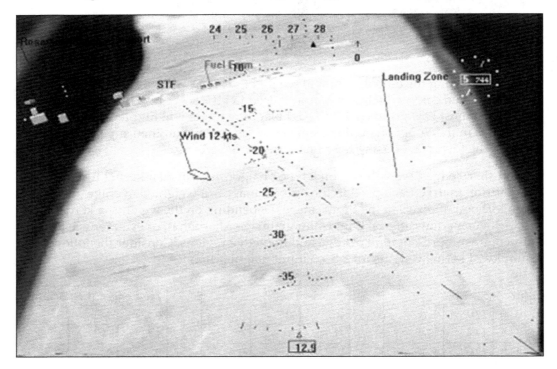

Here, we see navigational data and a simple map of a landing strip, superimposed on a live video feed from the drone. Due to cloud cover, the landing strip would be difficult to see in the original video, but thanks to AR, the strip is clearly marked. Thus, the remote pilot can guide the drone to a safe landing.

LightWork will not be a fully-fledged AR application, but the user will be able to superimpose images for artistic or practical purposes. We will explore AR further in *Chapter 4*, *Detecting and Merging Faces of Mammals*.

Planning the blending controls

We will add two more toolbar buttons, **Blend Src** and **Blend Mode**, to the lower-right corner of the app's main view. After launching LightWork, the user will see something like the following screenshot:

When the user clicks on **Blend Src**, a standard image picker will appear, as shown in the following screenshot:

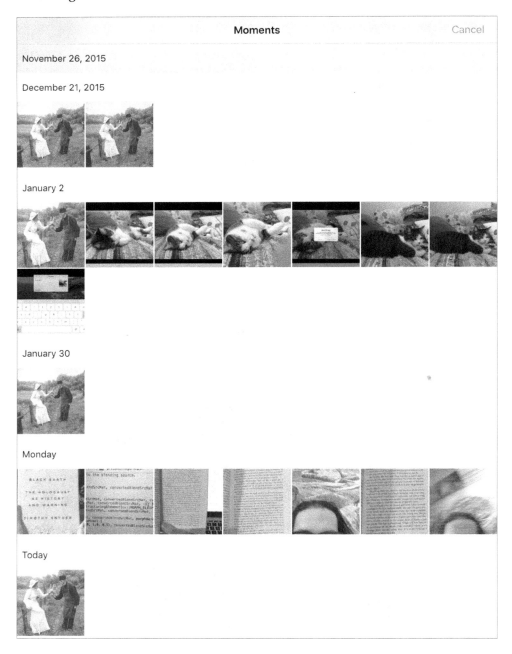

After the user picks an image, the app's main view will reappear and the user will see a blend of the selected foreground image and background image. By default, the blending mode will be a simple average of the foreground and background, as seen in the following screenshot:

When the user clicks on the **Blend Mode** button, a pop-up list of available blending modes will appear, as shown in the following screenshot:

The user may select any blending mode and, as usual, may press the switch camera button to select a live video feed as the background. For example, the following image was created with the **Multiply** blend mode and rear camera:

Here, the app has blended the face of Josephine (the gray and white cat) onto the back of Sanibel (the ginger cat). Both cats look bemused!

For examples of other blending modes and other types of images, see the *Using the application for practical purposes* section near the end of this chapter.

Expanding the view controller's interface

All of the new source code will go in `ViewController.m`. Open the file. After the import statements, let's define the following enumeration to identify the available blending modes:

```
enum BlendMode {
    None,
    Average,
    Multiply,
    Screen,
    HUD
};
```

Now, we need to add several new variables and methods to the private interface of our `ViewController` class. To provide callbacks to a standard image picker, our view controller must implement two protocols, `UIImagePickerControllerDelegate` and `UINavigationControllerDelegate`. We also need two more `cv::Mat` variables to store the selected foreground image in its original format and a converted format that is appropriate for the current background and blending mode. The blending mode is a variable, too. Note the highlighted changes in this block of code:

```
@interface ViewController () <CvVideoCameraDelegate,
    UIImagePickerControllerDelegate,
    UINavigationControllerDelegate> {
    cv::Mat originalStillMat;
    cv::Mat updatedStillMatGray;
    cv::Mat updatedStillMatRGBA;
    cv::Mat updatedVideoMatGray;
    cv::Mat updatedVideoMatRGBA;
    cv::Mat originalBlendSrcMat;
    cv::Mat convertedBlendSrcMat;

    BlendMode _blendMode;
}
```

We will treat the blending mode as an Objective-C property with a custom getter and setter. Later, in the setter's implementation, we will ensure that a Boolean property is also set every time the blending mode changes. Here are the properties' declarations:

```
@property BlendMode blendMode;
@property BOOL blendSettingsChanged;
```

Later, we will check the Boolean's value in the implementation of the `processImageHelper:` method to determine whether we need to recompute the initial stages of the blend. Remember that we wrote an empty implementation of `processImageHelper:` in *Chapter 2, Capturing, Storing, and Sharing Photos*. The method has the following signature:

```
- (void)processImageHelper:(cv::Mat &)mat;
```

For the **Blend Src** and **Blend Mode** toolbar buttons, we need two new `IBAction` callbacks. To anchor a pop-up to the **Blend Mode** button, we need a reference to the button, so we will make it an argument to the callback. Here are the callbacks' declarations:

```
- (IBAction)onBlendSrcButtonPressed;
- (IBAction)onBlendModeButtonPressed:(UIBarButtonItem *)sender;
```

As the pop-up menu will have several action buttons with similar functionality, we will use the following helper method to create each button:

```
- (UIAlertAction *)blendModeActionWithTitle:(NSString *)title
    blendMode:(BlendMode)blendMode;
```

Finally, let's add the following helper method, which will convert the foreground image to the appropriate size and color format:

```
- (void)convertBlendSrcMatToWidth:(int)dstW height:(int)dstH;

@end
```

Now that we have completed the modifications to the interface in
`ViewController.m`, let's open `Main.storyboard`. We need to add the **Blend Src**
and **Blend Mode** toolbar items after the second flexible space. Refer to the following
screenshot as a layout guide (or just download the completed storyboard from the
book's GitHub repository):

After completing the layout, we must connect the new toolbar buttons to the new IBAction hooks, which we defined in ViewController.m. Right-click on **View Controller** in the scene hierarchy to see the list of available outlets and actions. Set the connections so that they match the following screenshot:

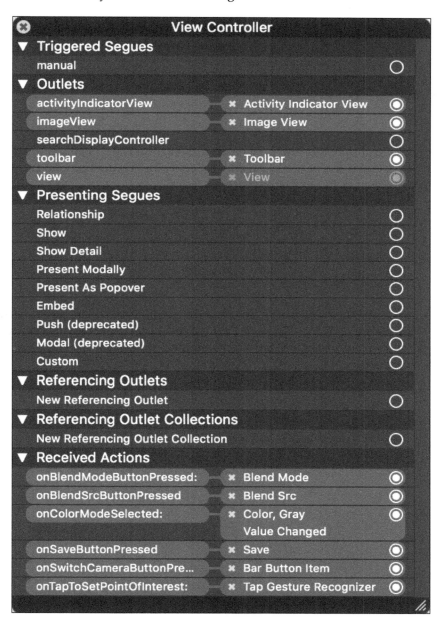

Expanding the view controller's implementation

Let's reopen `ViewController.m` to complete the implementation. First, let's add the custom getter and setter for the `blendMode` property. The getter will simply return the `_blendMode` variable, as seen in the following code:

```
@implementation ViewController

- (BlendMode)blendMode {
  return _blendMode;
}
```

The setter will check whether the new value differs from the old value. If so, the new value will be assigned to `_blendMode`, and the `blendSettingsChanged` property will be set to `YES`, as seen in the following code:

```
- (void)setBlendMode:(BlendMode)blendMode {
  if (blendMode != _blendMode) {
    _blendMode = blendMode;
    self.blendSettingsChanged = YES;
  }
}
```

Now, let's look at the new implementation of the `processImageHelper:` method. It is quite long, so we will consider it in four blocks. First, if the user has not yet selected any foreground image to blend, the method should return early, as shown in the following code:

```
- (void)processImageHelper:(cv::Mat &)mat {

  if (originalBlendSrcMat.empty()) {
    // No blending source has been selected.
    // Do nothing.
    return;
  }
```

Next, we need to ensure that the foreground image has received appropriate preprocessing. It must be converted to the same size and format as the background image. Also, we can precompute any part of the blending algorithm that depends on the foreground image alone. This way, fewer computations will occur on a per-frame basis when the background image changes. The following conditional statement checks whether new preprocessing is needed:

```
if (convertedBlendSrcMat.rows != mat.rows ||
    convertedBlendSrcMat.cols != mat.cols ||
    convertedBlendSrcMat.type() != mat.type() ||
    self.blendSettingsChanged) {
```

If new preprocessing is needed, first we call a helper method to resize the foreground image and convert its format. Then, we apply the foreground-specific part of the blending algorithm, which varies depending on the blending mode that the user has selected. At the end of the preprocessing, we set the blendSettingsChanged property to NO, as we have handled any change in the settings. Here is the relevant code:

```
// Resize the blending source and convert its format.
[self convertBlendSrcMatToWidth:mat.cols height:mat.rows];

// Apply any mode-dependent operations to the blending source.
switch (self.blendMode) {
  case Screen:
    /* Pseudocode:
     convertedBlendSrcMat = 255 - convertedBlendSrcMat;
     */
    cv::subtract(255.0, convertedBlendSrcMat,
      convertedBlendSrcMat);
    break;
  case HUD:
    /* Pseudocode:
     convertedBlendSrcMat =
       255 - Laplacian(GaussianBlur(convertedBlendSrcMat));
     */
    cv::GaussianBlur(convertedBlendSrcMat,
      convertedBlendSrcMat, cv::Size(5, 5), 0.0);
    cv::Laplacian(convertedBlendSrcMat, convertedBlendSrcMat,
      -1, 3);
    if (!self.videoCamera.grayscaleMode) {
      // The background is in color.
      // Give the foreground a yellowish green tint, which
      // will stand out against most backgrounds.
      cv::multiply(cv::Scalar(0.0, 1.0, 0.5),
```

```
        convertedBlendSrcMat, convertedBlendSrcMat);
      }
      cv::subtract(255.0, convertedBlendSrcMat,
        convertedBlendSrcMat);
      break;
    default:
      break;
  }

  self.blendSettingsChanged = NO;
}
```

To complete the `processImageHelper:` method, we blend the preprocessed foreground with the latest background image. Again, the algorithm varies depending on the blending mode that the user has selected. Here is the relevant code:

```
// Combine the blending source and the current frame.
switch (self.blendMode) {
  case Average:
    /* Pseudocode:
    mat = 0.5 * mat + 0.5 * convertedBlendSrcMat;
    */
    cv::addWeighted(mat, 0.5, convertedBlendSrcMat, 0.5, 0.0,
      mat);
    break;
  case Multiply:
    /* Pseudocode:
    mat = mat * convertedBlendSrcMat / 255;
    */
    cv::multiply(mat, convertedBlendSrcMat, mat, 1.0 / 255.0);
    break;
  case Screen:
  case HUD:
    /* Pseudocode:
    mat = 255 - (255 - mat) * convertedBlendSrcMat / 255;
    */
    cv::subtract(255.0, mat, mat);
    cv::multiply(mat, convertedBlendSrcMat, mat, 1.0 / 255.0);
    cv::subtract(255.0, mat, mat);
    break;
  default:
    break;
  }
}
```

For explanations of the blending algorithms, refer to the *Thinking about hybrid images* section at the beginning of this chapter.

When the user presses the **Blend Src** button, we will first check whether the Photos album is available. If it is unavailable, this probably means that the user refused to give LightWork access to Photos, and we will show an error alert and return. Otherwise, we will create a standard image picker, which is an instance of the UIImagePickerController class. To some extent, the picker is configurable. We will specify that our view controller is the picker's delegate, which provides callbacks. We will also tell the picker that we want to pick from the Photos album and require a still image (not a video). Finally, we will show the picker. Here is the **Blend Src** button's callback:

```
- (IBAction)onBlendSrcButtonPressed {

    if (![UIImagePickerController isSourceTypeAvailable:
        UIImagePickerControllerSourceTypeSavedPhotosAlbum]) {
      // The Photos album is unavailable.
      // Show an error message.
      UIAlertController *alert = [UIAlertController
        alertControllerWithTitle:@"Photos album unavailable"
        message:@"Go to the Settings app and give LightWork
        permission to access your Photos album."
        preferredStyle:UIAlertControllerStyleAlert];
      UIAlertAction *okAction = [UIAlertAction actionWithTitle:@"OK"
        style:UIAlertActionStyleDefault handler:nil];
      [alert addAction:okAction];
      [self presentViewController:alert animated:YES
        completion:nil];
      return;
    }

    UIImagePickerController *picker =
      [[UIImagePickerController alloc] init];
    picker.delegate = self;

    // Pick from the Photos album.
    picker.sourceType =
      UIImagePickerControllerSourceTypeSavedPhotosAlbum;

    // Pick from still images, not movies.
    picker.mediaTypes = [NSArray arrayWithObject:@"public.image"];

    [self presentViewController:picker animated:YES completion:nil];
}
```

As the image picker's delegate, our view controller is responsible for handling the user's interactions with the picker. We must even tell the picker when to dismiss itself. The UIImagePickerControllerDelegate protocol defines a callback to handle the user's selection of an image. The callback receives the image and other information about the user's choice in a dictionary called `info`. When the user picks an image, we will dismiss the picker. Then, we will get the image from the `info` dictionary and convert it to a `cv::Mat`. If no blending mode is selected, we will activate the `Average` mode. Finally, we will set our `blendSettingsChanged` property to `YES`. Here is the callback's implementation:

```
- (void)imagePickerController:(UIImagePickerController *)picker
    didFinishPickingMediaWithInfo:
      (NSDictionary<NSString *,id> *)info {
  [picker dismissViewControllerAnimated:YES completion:nil];

  UIImage *image =
    [info objectForKey:@"UIImagePickerControllerOriginalImage"];
  UIImageToMat(image, originalBlendSrcMat);

  if (self.blendMode == None) {
    // Blending is currently deactivated.
    // Activate "Average" blending so that the user sees some
    // result.
    self.blendMode = Average;
  }

  self.blendSettingsChanged = YES;
}
```

The UIImagePickerControllerDelegate protocol also defines a callback for the picker's cancel button. When the button is pressed, we will simply dismiss the picker, as seen in the following code:

```
- (void)imagePickerControllerDidCancel:
    (UIImagePickerController *)picker {
  [picker dismissViewControllerAnimated:YES completion:nil];
}
```

When the user presses the **Blend Mode** button, we will display a pop-up menu for the selection of a blending mode. The pop-up menu is just an alert that is configured to rise from the toolbar button. We will create each button with a helper method. Here is the implementation of the **Blend Mode** button's callback:

```
- (IBAction)onBlendModeButtonPressed:(UIBarButtonItem *)sender {
  UIAlertController *alert = [UIAlertController
```

```
      alertControllerWithTitle:nil message:nil
        preferredStyle:UIAlertControllerStyleActionSheet];
    alert.popoverPresentationController.barButtonItem = sender;

    UIAlertAction *averageAction = [self
      blendModeActionWithTitle:@"Average" blendMode:Average];
    [alert addAction:averageAction];

    UIAlertAction *multiplyAction = [self
      blendModeActionWithTitle:@"Multiply" blendMode:Multiply];
    [alert addAction:multiplyAction];

    UIAlertAction *screenAction = [self
      blendModeActionWithTitle:@"Screen" blendMode:Screen];
    [alert addAction:screenAction];

    UIAlertAction *hudAction = [self
      blendModeActionWithTitle:@"HUD" blendMode:HUD];
    [alert addAction:hudAction];

    UIAlertAction *noneAction = [self
      blendModeActionWithTitle:@"None" blendMode:None];
    [alert addAction:noneAction];

    [self presentViewController:alert animated:YES completion:nil];
}
```

When the user presses a button in the pop-up menu, we set our `blendMode` property to the appropriate value. Also, if the static background is active, we refresh it. Here is the helper method that creates a menu button and its callback:

```
- (UIAlertAction *)blendModeActionWithTitle:(NSString *)title
    blendMode:(BlendMode)blendMode {
  UIAlertAction *action = [UIAlertAction actionWithTitle:title
    style:UIAlertActionStyleDefault
    handler:^(UIAlertAction * _Nonnull action) {
      self.blendMode = blendMode;
      if (!self.videoCamera.running) {
        [self refresh];
      }
    }];
  return action;
}
```

Finally, let's look at the helper method that converts the foreground image to match the size and format of the background image. First, we select a subregion of the foreground image to match the background's aspect ratio. Then, we resize this subregion using a high-quality interpolation algorithm called **Lanczos**. We finish by converting the resized image to either a grayscale or BGRA format. Here is the implementation:

```
- (void)convertBlendSrcMatToWidth:(int)dstW height:(int)dstH {

    double dstAspectRatio = dstW / (double)dstH;

    int srcW = originalBlendSrcMat.cols;
    int srcH = originalBlendSrcMat.rows;
    double srcAspectRatio = srcW / (double)srcH;
    cv::Mat subMat;
    if (srcAspectRatio < dstAspectRatio) {
        int subMatH = (int)(srcW / dstAspectRatio);
        int startRow = (srcH - subMatH) / 2;
        int endRow = startRow + subMatH;
        subMat = originalBlendSrcMat.rowRange(startRow, endRow);
    } else {
        int subMatW = (int)(srcH * dstAspectRatio);
        int startCol = (srcW - subMatW) / 2;
        int endCol = startCol + subMatW;
        subMat = originalBlendSrcMat.colRange(startCol, endCol);
    }
    cv::resize(subMat, convertedBlendSrcMat, cv::Size(dstW, dstH),
        0.0, 0.0, cv::INTER_LANCZOS4);

    int cvtColorCode;
    if (self.videoCamera.grayscaleMode) {
        cvtColorCode = cv::COLOR_RGBA2GRAY;
    } else {
        cvtColorCode = cv::COLOR_RGBA2BGRA;
    }
    cv::cvtColor(convertedBlendSrcMat, convertedBlendSrcMat,
        cvtColorCode);
}

@end
```

At this point, the new version of LightWork is complete, and we can build and run it.

Using the application for practical purposes

Although LightWork's design and algorithms are rather simple, it is a versatile tool in the hands of a crafty user. For example, with the use of our blending filters, we can accomplish any task in the following broad categories:

- See how a scene has changed over time
- Before actually building or moving an object, visualize how it would look in a scene
- Before actually copying a document or drawing, visualize how it would look on a different surface

Let's consider each category in pictures.

Seeing changes in a scene

This requires a few steps of preparation:

1. Set up the smartphone or tablet in a stable position. For example, mount it on a tripod.
2. Point the camera at an area where you expect movement to occur.
3. Open the LightWork app, activate the rear-facing camera, and save a picture.
4. Click on **Blend Src** and select the picture that you just saved.
5. Click on **Blend Mode** and select **Average**, **Screen**, or **Multiply**.
6. Watch the live video to see a blend of the past and present.

Consider the following series of images, which show a construction site on a windy winter day. Here, I used the leftmost image as **Blend Src** and I selected the **Average** blending mode. The second image is a blending result that shows a piece of paper blowing in the wind in the middle-right window. The rightmost image is another blending result that shows a man moving in the foreground. Note that the moving objects appear to be semi-transparent:

Over a longer period of time, we would also start to see the semi-transparent effect in slowly moving objects, such as the snowdrifts.

Previewing a new object in a scene

For this, we require a real object, but it may be a scale model. Take a photo of the object on a light background and use it with the **Multiply** blending mode. Alternatively, take a photo on a dark background and use it with the **Screen** blending mode. Go to the scene and see how the object looks in the live video.

Let's consider a case study. Jan is an artist and interior decorator. She creates her art by hand, not with digital technology. Sometimes, she makes gigantic stuffed animals for children and cats. *Yes, cats like stuffed animals, too.* Suppose that Jan wants to take a photo of a child's favorite stuffed animal and show the child and parents how a similar creature might look on a bigger scale. With LightWork, she could capture the first image in the following pair of images and create the second image as part of a live preview:

Here, the **Multiply** blending mode works quite well to produce a coherent image, except in the dark region of the bed's headboard. With the real-time video preview, the user can work around these localized flaws by moving to get different perspectives. Most importantly, this type of visualization is mobile, fast, and does not require skill in digital image editing. Jan can use this to give other people an immediate preview of the things she imagines.

Previewing a copy of a document or drawing

For this, we require a document or drawing with sharp letters or shapes. Capture a photo of the document or drawing and use it with the **HUD** blending mode. Point the camera at a blank surface so that you can see the outlines of the letters or shapes. You may want to stabilize the iOS device so that the outlines do not move. For example, see the improvised stabilization in the following photo, where an iPad Mini is suspended over a sheet of black construction paper:

Now, consider the following two images, which show a verse from a famous Russian poem called *Ochi chyornye* (*Black Eyes* or *Dark Eyes*). The author is Yevhen Hrebinka, a 19th-century Ukrainian romantic writer. The top image is the original document and the bottom image is the virtual stencil with the **HUD** effect:

Here, the virtual stencil might be particularly useful for an English speaker who is just learning the Russian Cyrillic alphabet or a Russian speaker who is just learning the Latin alphabet. That is to say, an unfamiliar alphabet could make it more difficult for a person to simply imagine how a copy of the document would look.

Summary

We have completed the LightWork application by adding a set of image blending options. Moreover, we have considered the notion that an image represents a slice of time and space, so a blended image creates a hybrid time and hybrid space. Photographers might think of this hybridization as *multiple exposure*, while app designers might call it **augmented reality** (**AR**). Starting in the next chapter, we will explore more sophisticated AR techniques, which involve detecting and tracking an object in the live video and superimposing other graphics to precisely fit the object's features.

4
Detecting and Merging Faces of Mammals

"A cat may look at a king."

– English proverb

This chapter puts a spotlight on two of my favorite subjects: cats and **augmented reality (AR)**. We will build an AR application called ManyMasks, which will detect, highlight, and merge the faces of humans and cats. Specifically, the app's user will be able to do the following things:

- See the boundaries of a human face or cat face in a live camera view as well as the centers of the eyes and the tip of the nose. This visualization depends on the result of a face detection algorithm.
- Select two detected faces from different camera frames.
- See a hybrid face, which is produced by aligning and blending the two selected faces.
- Save and share the hybrid face.

Our face detection algorithm relies on **cascade classifiers**, which attempt to match various patches of the image to a pretrained, generic model of a human face, human eye, or cat face. We estimate the positions of other facial features based on a set of geometric assumptions about the structure of a face.

Our face merging algorithm relies on a geometric transformation, which may rotate and warp one face to align its features with those of another face. Then, we just arithmetically blend the pixels of the aligned images.

Although we will design ManyMasks to work on humans and cats, it may detect and merge other mammals too. The following images show you how the app merges me with my father Bob (left), my cat Sanibel (upper right), and a red panda (lower right):

 To obtain the completed projects for this book, you can refer to my GitHub repository at https://github.com/JoeHowse/iOSWithOpenCV or log in to your account on Packt Publishing's site at https://www.packtpub.com/. The project for *Chapter 4, Detecting and Merging Faces of Mammals*, is in the ManyMasks subfolder.

Understanding detection with cascade classifiers

A **cascade** is a series of tests or stages, which differentiate between a positive and negative class of objects, such as *face* and *non-face*. For a positive classification, a patch of an image must pass all stages of the cascade. Conversely, if the patch fails any stage, the classifier immediately makes a negative classification.

A **patch** or **window** of an image is a sample of pixels around a given position and at a given magnification level. A cascade classifier takes windows of the image at various positions and various magnification levels, and for each window it runs the stages of the cascade. Often, positive detections occur in multiple, overlapping windows. These overlapping positive detections are called **neighbors**, and they imply a greater likelihood of a true positive. For example, a real face still looks like a face if we move or resize the frame around it slightly.

By now, you might be wondering exactly how we design a cascade's stages. The answer is, we do not directly design them. Rather, we let a machine learning meta-algorithm design the stages based on a set of training images and a set of features. Typically, the meta-algorithm is a variant of **AdaBoost** (**adaptive boosting**), which is a form of linear regression with a specialized exponential error function. The training images include positive samples and negative samples, and we must provide the metadata about the coordinates of objects in the positive samples. The features are templates of local patterns that the classifier may (or may not) find in each neighborhood. The training algorithm selects features that are typical of positive samples and atypical of negative samples, and it designs the stages based on these selections.

Haar-like features

Haar-like features are one of the most popular kinds of features used for face detection, and for object detection in general. For each window, a Haar cascade classifier subtracts some of the grayscale pixel values from others in order to measure the window's similarity to the following features, where a dark region meets a light region:

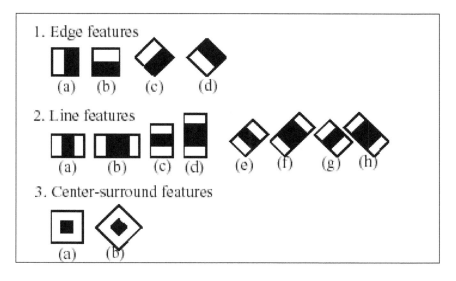

Thus, the stages of the Haar cascade represent horizontal or diagonal edges, thin lines, or dots that typify an object (versus a non-object). Some variants of the algorithm remove features (such as the diagonal features) or add features (such as corners where four rectangles meet), but the basic idea is the same.

Haar-like features are not robust with respect to rotation or flipping. For example, if a Haar cascade is trained to detect upright faces, it will not detect upside-down faces. Similarly, if a Haar cascade is trained for a left eye, it is not ideal for a right eye, which is a mirror image of the left eye. Thus, it is better to have separate cascades for left and right eyes. We will use four pretrained Haar cascades that come with OpenCV, and these cascades will detect an upright human face, an upright cat face, a human left eye, and a human right eye.

Local binary pattern features

Local binary pattern (LBP) features are another popular kind of feature. They are also called **local binary pattern histogram** (LBPH) features. As the name suggests, an LBPH feature is a histogram or count of brightness values. For each pixel in a window, the classifier notes whether each neighboring pixel in a certain radius is brighter or darker. The histogram holds a count of the darker pixels in each neighboring position. For example, suppose a window contains the following two neighborhoods of 1-pixel radius:

Black	White	Black
White	White	White
Black	White	Black

Black	Black	Black
White	White	White
White	White	White

Counting these two neighborhoods (and not yet counting other neighborhoods in the window), the histogram can be visualized like this:

2	1	2
0	0	0
1	0	1

Let's review how we arrived at these figures. The first neighborhood has dark corners (relative to the center), so we add 1 to each corner cell of the histogram table. The second neighborhood has a dark top row (relative to the center), so we add another 1 to each cell in the top row of the histogram table.

The stages of the LBP cascade represent gradients or transitions that typify an object (versus a non-object).

Like Haar cascades, LBP cascades are not robust with respect to rotation or flipping. OpenCV comes with pretrained LBP cascades for an upright human face and upright cat face. Optionally, we can use these instead of the Haar cascades.

Compared to Haar cascades, LBP cascades tend to offer faster but less accurate detection results. For low-end devices, or in cases where high frame rates are required, LBP cascades may be a good choice. However, recent iOS devices are quite capable of using Haar cascades with live video.

 For information on OpenCV's implementation of cascade classifiers, see the official documentation at `http://docs.opencv.org/3.1.0/d5/d54/group__objdetect.html`. Specifically, we will use the `cv::CascadeClassifier` class.

Understanding transformations

After we detect two faces and before we blend them, we will try to align the faces based on the eye and nose coordinates. This alignment step is a geometric transformation, which remaps points (or pixels) from one space to another. For example, the following geometric operations are special cases of a transformation:

- **Translation:** This moves the points laterally. It repositions them around a new center.
- **Rotation:** This spins the points around a center.
- **Scale:** This moves the points farther from or nearer to a center.

Mathematically, a transformation is a matrix and a point (or pixel position) is a vector. We can multiply them together to apply the transformation to the point. The output of the multiplication is a new point.

Conversely, given three pairs of points — in our case, the pairs of left eye centers, right eye centers, and nose tips — we can solve for the transformation matrix that maps one set of points onto the other. This is a problem of linear algebra. After finding the matrix, we will apply it to a whole face, not just the eyes and nose.

For information on the OpenCV functions that find and apply transformation matrices, see the official documentation at `http://docs.opencv.org/3.1.0/da/d54/group__` `imgproc__transform.html`. Specifically, we will use the `cv::getAffineTransformation` and `cv::warpAffine` functions.

Planning a face merging application

When ManyMasks opens, it will present a live camera view, a toolbar, and two small images of a masked face in the lower corners. Whenever the application detects a human face, it will draw the following shapes:

- A yellow rectangle around the face region
- A red rectangle around the left eye region
- A red circle at the left eye's center or pupil
- A green rectangle around the right eye region
- A green circle at the right eye's center or pupil
- A blue circle at the tip of the nose

Similarly, for a detected cat face, the application will draw the following shapes:

- A white rectangle around the face region
- A red circle at the left eye's center or pupil
- A green circle at the right eye's center or pupil
- A blue circle at the tip of the nose

 For our purposes, the left and right directions refer to the viewer's perspective, not the subject's perspective. The OpenCV developers, and most authors in computer vision, also follow this convention.

The following screenshot shows how the application might look at startup if the user's face is detected:

The toolbar provides a segmented control to select a color mode and switch camera button to select the front or rear camera. These controls are similar to the ones we implemented in *Chapter 2, Capturing, Storing, and Sharing Photos*, so we will not say much about them in this chapter.

Beside the camera controls, the toolbar provides three more buttons. The **Face 1** and **Face 2** buttons enable the user to select the currently detected face. (If there is more than one currently detected face, the largest is selected.) The selected faces appear in the small image views in the lower corners, as seen in the following screenshot:

After selecting two faces, the user may press the **Merge** button. Then, the application presents a modal view controller, showing a hybrid face and a different toolbar, like the following screenshot:

On the left side, the toolbar contains a standard trash button, which discards the image and takes the user back to the camera view. On the right side, there is a **Save** button, which stores the image in the user's Photos album and prompts the user about posting the image to a social network. For example, if a user has a Twitter account on the device, the following dialog will appear:

If the user opts to share the image, a standard composition dialog will appear, as shown in the following screenshot:

Remember that we implemented similar functionality to save and share images in *Chapter 2, Capturing, Storing, and Sharing Photos*. Thus, we will not say much about it in this chapter.

After the user shares the image or opts not to share it, the application will return to the camera view. Then, the user may select and merge faces again.

Configuring the project

Create an Xcode project named ManyMasks. Use the **Single View Application** template. Configure the project according to the instructions in *Chapter 1, Setting Up Software and Hardware* and *Chapter 2, Capturing, Storing, and Sharing Photos*. (See the *Configuring the project* section of each chapter.) The ManyMasks project depends on the same frameworks and device capabilities as the LightWork project.

Our face detector will depend on several pretrained cascade files that come with OpenCV's source code. If you do not already have the source code, get it as described in *Chapter 1, Setting Up Software and Hardware*, in the *Building an additional framework from source with extra modules* section. Add copies of the following cascade files to the Supporting Files folder of the ManyMasks project:

- `<opencv_source_path>/data/haarcascades/haarcascade_frontalface_alt.xml`. Alternatively, you may want to try `<opencv_source_path>/data/lbpcascades/lbpcascade_frontalface.xml` for faster but less accurate results.
- `<opencv_source_path>/data/haarcascades/haarcascade_frontalcatface_extended.xml`. Alternatively, you may want to try `<opencv_source_path>/data/lbpcascades/lbpcascade_frontalcatface.xml` for faster but less accurate results.
- `<opencv_source_path>/data/haarcascades/haarcascade_lefteye_2splits.xml`
- `<opencv_source_path>/data/haarcascades/haarcascade_righteye_2splits.xml`

After adding the cascade files, select **ManyMasks** in the project navigator pane. Open the **Build Phases** tab in the editor area, and make sure that the four cascade files appear in the **Copy Bundle Resources** list.

 For a detailed description of how the `*_frontalcatface*.xml` cascade files were trained, see *Chapter 3, Training a Smart Alarm to Recognize the Villain and His Cat* in my book, *OpenCV for Secret Agents*, (Packt Publishing, 2015).

Defining faces and a face detector

Let's define faces and a face detector in pure C++ code without using any dependencies except OpenCV. This ensures that the computer vision functionality of ManyMasks is portable. We could reuse the core of our code on a different platform with a different set of UI libraries.

A face has a species. For our purposes, this could be `Human`, `Cat`, or `Hybrid`. Let's create a header file, `Species.h`, and define the following `enum` in it:

```
#ifndef SPECIES_H
#define SPECIES_H

enum Species {
  Human,
  Cat,
  Hybrid
};

#endif // !SPECIES_H
```

A face also has a matrix of image data and three feature points representing the centers of the eyes and tip of the nose. We may construct a face in any of the following ways:

*   Specify a species, matrix, and feature points.
*   Create an empty face with default values, including an empty matrix.
*   Copy an existing face.
*   Merge two existing faces.

Let's create another header file, `Face.h`, and declare the following public interface of a `Face` class in it:

```
#ifndef FACE_H
#define FACE_H

#include <opencv2/core.hpp>

#include "Species.h"

class Face {

public:
  Face(Species species, const cv::Mat &mat,
```

```
        const cv::Point2f &leftEyeCenter,
        const cv::Point2f &rightEyeCenter,
        const cv::Point2f &noseTip);

    /**
     * Construct an empty face.
     */
    Face();

    /**
     * Construct a face by copying another face.
     */
    Face(const Face &other);

    /**
     * Construct a face by merging two other faces.
     */
    Face(const Face &face0, const Face &face1);

    bool isEmpty() const;

    Species getSpecies() const;

    const cv::Mat &getMat() const;
    int getWidth() const;
    int getHeight() const;

    const cv::Point2f &getLeftEyeCenter() const;
    const cv::Point2f &getRightEyeCenter() const;
    const cv::Point2f &getNoseTip() const;
```

Note that Face is designed as an **immutable** type, meaning that its properties shall not change after construction. To help enforce this, we add the const keyword at the end of method declarations. The use of immutable types can help make code safe, predictable, and elegant because an object is **stateless** (or more precisely, its current state remains the same as its initial state). Callers can assign a copy of a face (via the copy constructor) but cannot rearrange elements of an existing face. ManyMasks is an artistic app, not a gangster movie; we construct faces, we don't rearrange them.

The Face class's private interface defines the expected variables as well as a method to help construct merged faces. Here is the relevant code, which completes Face.h:

```
    private:
        void initMergedFace(const Face &biggerFace,
```

```
    const Face &smallerFace);

  Species species;

  cv::Mat mat;

  cv::Point2f leftEyeCenter;
  cv::Point2f rightEyeCenter;
  cv::Point2f noseTip;
};

#endif // !FACE_H
```

Our face detector has cascade classifiers for a human face, left and right human eyes, and a cat face. The constructor takes paths to the relevant cascade files. After it is constructed, a face detector's role is simply to detect faces! A `detect` function accepts the current image of the scene along with a `vector<Face>` to populate with results. Optionally, the caller may also specify that the detector should process a resized image and that it should draw a visualization of the detection results on the original image. The optional visualization consists of rectangles and circles that show the detected face, eye, and nose positions. Let's create yet another header file, `FaceDetector.h`, and declare the following public interface of the `FaceDetector` class in it:

```
#ifndef FACE_DETECTOR_H
#define FACE_DETECTOR_H

#include <opencv2/objdetect.hpp>

#include "Face.h"

class FaceDetector {

public:
  FaceDetector(const std::string &humanFaceCascadePath,
    const std::string &catFaceCascadePath,
    const std::string &humanLeftEyeCascadePath,
    const std::string &humanRightEyeCascadePath);

  void detect(cv::Mat &image, std::vector<Face> &faces,
    double resizeFactor = 1.0, bool draw = false);
```

The private interface declares several variables as well as helper methods to equalize the image (that is, to standardize its contrast) and detect the eyes and nose. Equalization helps to ensure consistent detection results under various lighting conditions. Here is the relevant code, which completes `FaceDetector.h`:

```
private:
  void equalize(const cv::Mat &image);
  void detectInnerComponents(const cv::Mat &image,
    std::vector<Face> &faces, double resizeFactor, bool draw,
    Species species, cv::Rect faceRect);

  cv::CascadeClassifier humanFaceClassifier;
  cv::CascadeClassifier catFaceClassifier;
  cv::CascadeClassifier humanLeftEyeClassifier;
  cv::CascadeClassifier humanRightEyeClassifier;

#ifdef WITH_CLAHE
  cv::Ptr<cv::CLAHE> clahe;
#endif

  cv::Mat resizedImage;
  cv::Mat equalizedImage;
};

#endif // !FACE_DETECTOR_H
```

 Note the use of a preprocessor condition, `WITH_CLAHE`. If we define `WITH_CLAHE` in the **Preprocessor Macros** section of our project's **Build Settings**, our face detector will take advantage of an advanced equalization algorithm called **contrast limited adaptive histogram equalization (CLAHE)**. Otherwise, it will use a cheaper but less robust equalization algorithm.

Later in this chapter, in the *Detecting a hierarchy of face elements* and *Aligning and blending face elements* sections, we will examine noteworthy implementation details that belong in other files, `Face.cpp` and `FaceDetector.cpp`. First, though, let's consider the view controllers that use faces and face detection.

Defining and laying out the view controllers

ManyMasks divides its application logic between two view controllers. The first view controller enables the user to capture and preview real faces. The second enables the user to review, save, and share merged faces. A type of callback method called a **segue** enables the first view controller to instantiate the second and pass a merged face to it.

Capturing and previewing real faces

Import copies of the `VideoCamera.h` and `VideoCamera.m` files that we created in *Chapter 2, Capturing, Storing, and Sharing Photos*. These files contain our `VideoCamera` class, which extends OpenCV's `CvVideoCamera` to fix bugs and add new functionality.

Rename `ViewController.h` and `ViewController.m` to `CaptureViewController.h` and `CaptureViewController.m`. Edit `CaptureViewController.h` so that it declares a `CaptureViewController` class, as seen in the following code:

```
#import <UIKit/UIKit.h>

@interface CaptureViewController : UIViewController

@end
```

`CaptureViewController` will have similarities to `ViewController` *Chapter 2, Capturing, Storing, and Sharing Photos*. Basically, both classes control a camera and process images. Edit `CaptureViewController.m` so that it declares the following private interface for `CaptureViewController`:

```
#import <opencv2/core.hpp>
#import <opencv2/imgcodecs/ios.h>
#import <opencv2/imgproc.hpp>

#import "CaptureViewController.h"
#import "FaceDetector.h"
#import "ReviewViewController.h"
#import "VideoCamera.h"

const double DETECT_RESIZE_FACTOR = 0.5;

@interface CaptureViewController () <CvVideoCameraDelegate> {
```

```
    FaceDetector *faceDetector;
    std::vector<Face> detectedFaces;
    Face bestDetectedFace;
    Face faceToMerge0;
    Face faceToMerge1;
}

@property IBOutlet UIView *backgroundView;

@property IBOutlet UIBarButtonItem *face0Button;
@property IBOutlet UIBarButtonItem *face1Button;
@property IBOutlet UIBarButtonItem *mergeButton;

@property IBOutlet UIImageView *face0ImageView;
@property IBOutlet UIImageView *face1ImageView;

@property VideoCamera *videoCamera;

- (IBAction)onTapToSetPointOfInterest:
    (UITapGestureRecognizer *)tapGesture;
- (IBAction)onColorModeSelected:
    (UISegmentedControl *)segmentedControl;
- (IBAction)onSwitchCameraButtonPressed;
- (IBAction)onFace0ButtonPressed;
- (IBAction)onFace1ButtonPressed;

- (void)refresh;
- (void)processImage:(cv::Mat &)mat;
- (void)showFace:(Face &)face inImageView:
    (UIImageView *)imageView;
- (UIImage *)imageFromCapturedMat:(const cv::Mat &)mat;

@end
```

 Note that `CaptureViewController` has a `FaceDetector` pointer and a vector of `Face` objects representing the currently detected faces. It also has three more `Face` variables to keep track of the best (largest) currently detected face and the two previously selected faces. The remainder of the private interface pertains to GUI elements, camera control, and image processing.

As usual, the `viewDidLoad` method is responsible for initializing variables. The constructor of `FaceDetector` requires the paths to the four cascade files in the application's main resource bundle. Note how we obtain the paths in the following code:

```objc
- (void)viewDidLoad {
  [super viewDidLoad];

  if (faceDetector == NULL) {

    NSBundle *bundle = [NSBundle mainBundle];

    std::string humanFaceCascadePath = [[bundle
      pathForResource:@"haarcascade_frontalface_alt"
      ofType:@"xml"] UTF8String];
    std::string catFaceCascadePath = [[bundle
      pathForResource:@"haarcascade_frontalcatface_extended"
      ofType:@"xml"] UTF8String];
    std::string leftEyeCascadePath = [[bundle
      pathForResource:@"haarcascade_lefteye_2splits"
      ofType:@"xml"] UTF8String];
    std::string rightEyeCascadePath = [[bundle
      pathForResource:@"haarcascade_righteye_2splits"
      ofType:@"xml"] UTF8String];

    faceDetector = new FaceDetector(humanFaceCascadePath,
      catFaceCascadePath, leftEyeCascadePath,
      rightEyeCascadePath);
  }

  self.face0Button.enabled = NO;
  self.face1Button.enabled = NO;
  self.mergeButton.enabled = (!faceToMerge0.isEmpty() &&
    !faceToMerge1.isEmpty());

  self.videoCamera = [[VideoCamera alloc]
    initWithParentView:self.backgroundView];
  self.videoCamera.delegate = self;
  self.videoCamera.defaultAVCaptureSessionPreset =
    AVCaptureSessionPresetHigh;
  self.videoCamera.defaultFPS = 30;
  self.videoCamera.letterboxPreview = YES;
}
```

The `FaceDetector` object loads the four cascade files into memory, so its resource requirements are significant. Moreover, iOS does not provide automatic memory management for this dynamically allocated C++ object. Let's override the following `UIViewController` methods to ensure that the face detector is deleted when the system is running out of memory or when the view controller itself is deallocated:

```
- (void)didReceiveMemoryWarning {
  [super didReceiveMemoryWarning];

  if (faceDetector != NULL) {
    delete faceDetector;
    faceDetector = NULL;
  }
}

- (void)dealloc {
  if (faceDetector != NULL) {
    delete faceDetector;
    faceDetector = NULL;
  }
}
```

 If the system calls `didReceiveMemoryWarning`, it will subsequently call `viewDidLoad` before presenting the view controller again. Thus, we can be confident that the face detector will be recreated in a timely manner.

Every time the camera captures a new frame, we will pass the frame to the face detector. We will also specify that the detector should scale down the image to half its original size. (We defined this scaling factor at the top of the file as a constant.) If any faces are detected, we will keep a copy of the best (largest) detected face and enable the **Face 0** and **Face 1** buttons so that the user may select this face. Otherwise, we will disable these buttons. Here is the relevant code in the `processImage` callback:

```
- (void)processImage:(cv::Mat &)mat {

  switch (self.videoCamera.defaultAVCaptureVideoOrientation) {
    case AVCaptureVideoOrientationLandscapeLeft:
    case AVCaptureVideoOrientationLandscapeRight:
      // The landscape video is captured upside-down.
      // Rotate it by 180 degrees.
      cv::flip(mat, mat, -1);
      break;
    default:
```

```
      break;
  }

  // Detect and draw any faces.
  faceDetector->detect(mat, detectedFaces, DETECT_RESIZE_FACTOR,
    true);

  BOOL didDetectFaces = (detectedFaces.size() > 0);

  if (didDetectFaces) {
    if (didDetectFaces) {
      // Find the biggest face.
      int bestFaceIndex = 0;
      for (int i = 0, bestFaceArea = 0;
          i < detectedFaces.size(); i++) {
        Face &detectedFace = detectedFaces[i];
        int faceArea = detectedFace.getWidth() *
          detectedFace.getHeight();
        if (faceArea > bestFaceArea) {
          bestFaceIndex = i;
          bestFaceArea = faceArea;
        }
      }
      bestDetectedFace = detectedFaces[bestFaceIndex];
    }
  }

  dispatch_async(dispatch_get_main_queue(), ^{
    self.face0Button.enabled = didDetectFaces;
    self.face1Button.enabled = didDetectFaces;
  });
}
```

When the user presses the **Face 0** or **Face 1** button, we will copy the best currently detected face to another variable and show a thumbnail of the face. Here is the relevant callback for the **Face 0** button:

```
- (IBAction)onFace0ButtonPressed {
    faceToMerge0 = bestDetectedFace;
    [self showFace:faceToMerge0 inImageView:self.face0ImageView];
    if (!faceToMerge1.isEmpty()) {
        dispatch_async(dispatch_get_main_queue(), ^{
            self.mergeButton.enabled = YES;
        });
    }
}
```

Of course, the callback for the **Face 1** button is similar. The following two helper methods actually implement the logic of getting the face's image and converting it to an appropriate format:

```
- (void)showFace:(Face &)face
    inImageView:(UIImageView *)imageView {
  imageView.image = [self imageFromCapturedMat:face.getMat()];
}

- (UIImage *)imageFromCapturedMat:(const cv::Mat &)mat {
  switch (mat.channels()) {
    case 4: {
      cv::Mat rgbMat;
      cv::cvtColor(mat, rgbMat, cv::COLOR_BGRA2RGB);
      return MatToUIImage(rgbMat);
    }
    default:
      // The source is grayscale.
      return MatToUIImage(mat);
  }
}
```

 For the implementation of the **Merge** button's action, see the *Seguing between the view controllers* section later in this chapter.

Now that we have examined the interface and some of the interesting implementation details in `CaptureViewController.m`, let's open `Main.storyboard`. Select **View Controller** in the scene hierarchy. Go to the inspector pane's **Identity** tab. (Its icon looks like a document containing a picture and text.) Set the **Class** of the view controller to **CaptureViewController**, as shown in the following screenshot:

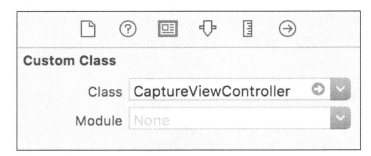

Now, let's add the appropriate GUI widgets as children of the view controller's main view. Refer to the following screenshot as a layout guide (or just download the completed storyboard from the book's GitHub repository):

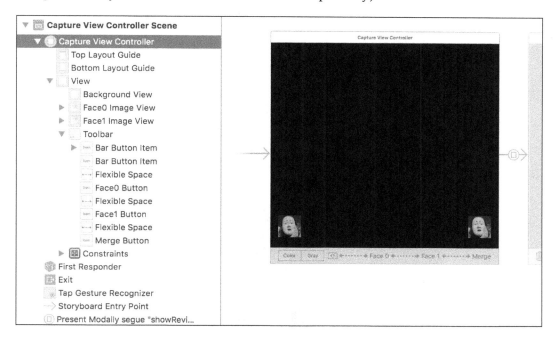

Right-click on **Capture View Controller** in the scene hierarchy to see the list of available outlets and actions, which we defined in CaptureViewController.m. Set the connections so that they match the following screenshot:

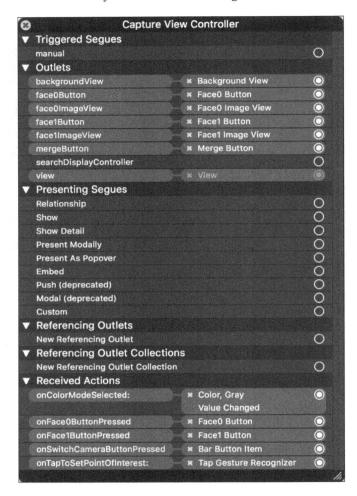

Reviewing, saving, and sharing hybrid faces

Add two new files, ReviewViewController.h and ReviewViewController.m. Edit ReviewViewController.h so that it declares a ReviewViewController class with a UIImage as a property. Here is the relevant code:

```
#import <UIKit/UIKit.h>

@interface ReviewViewController : UIViewController
```

```
@property UIImage *image;

@end
```

Note that the `image` property is part of the class's public interface. Our other view controller, `CaptureViewController`, will set this property in order to provide an image of a merged face.

Now, edit `ReviewViewController.m` to add the class's private interface. It contains callbacks for the trash and **Save** buttons as well as several helper methods to save and share images. We have already seen most of this functionality in the `ViewController` class in *Chapter 2, Capturing, Storing, and Sharing Photos*. Here is the start of the code in `ReviewViewController.m`:

```
#import <Photos/Photos.h>
#import <Social/Social.h>

#import "ReviewViewController.h"

@interface ReviewViewController ()

@property IBOutlet UIImageView *imageView;
@property IBOutlet UIActivityIndicatorView *activityIndicatorView;
@property IBOutlet UIToolbar *toolbar;

- (IBAction)onDeleteButtonPressed;
- (IBAction)onSaveButtonPressed;

- (void)saveImage:(UIImage *)image;
- (void)showSaveImageFailureAlertWithMessage:(NSString *)message;
- (void)showSaveImageSuccessAlertWithImage:(UIImage *)image;
- (UIAlertAction *)shareImageActionWithTitle:(NSString *)title
    serviceType:(NSString *)serviceType image:(UIImage *)image;
- (void)startBusyMode;
- (void)stopBusyMode;

@end
```

By the time `ReviewViewController` loads its view, the previous view controller should have already set the `image` property. To initialize the view, `ReviewViewController` just needs to show the image. Here is the relevant code:

```
- (void)viewDidLoad {
  [super viewDidLoad];

  self.imageView.image = self.image;
}
```

If the user presses the "trash" button, `ReviewViewController` simply dismisses itself without saving or sharing the image:

```
- (IBAction)onDeleteButtonPressed {
    [self dismissViewControllerAnimated:YES completion:nil];
}
```

Alternatively, if the user presses the **Save** button, `ReviewViewController` shows a busy indicator, disables the toolbar items, saves the image, offers options to share the image, and finally dismisses itself. The button's callback has a two-line implementation, as it relies on helper methods like the ones we implemented in *Chapter 2, Capturing, Storing, and Sharing Photos*:

```
- (IBAction)onSaveButtonPressed {
    [self startBusyMode];
    [self saveImage:self.image];
}
```

Now that we have examined the interface and some of the interesting implementation details in `ReviewViewController.m`, let's open `Main.storyboard`. Drag a new view controller from the library pane to the editor area. Select the new **View Controller** in the scene hierarchy. Go to the inspector pane's **Identity** tab (its icon looks like a document containing a picture and text). Set the **Class** of the view controller to **ReviewViewController**, as shown in the following screenshot:

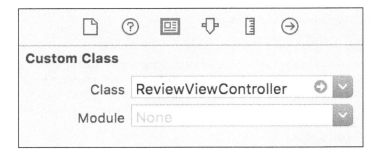

Now, let's add the appropriate GUI widgets as children of the view controller's main view. Refer to the following screenshot as a layout guide (or just download the completed storyboard from the book's GitHub repository):

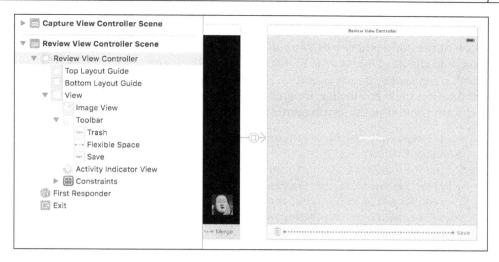

Right-click on **Review View Controller** in the scene hierarchy to see the list of available outlets and actions, which we defined in `ReviewViewController.m`. Set the connections so that they match the following screenshot:

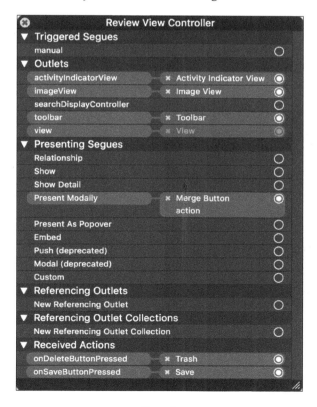

Seguing between the view controllers

Let's look at the code where our CaptureViewController provides the merged face image to the ReviewViewController. The UIViewController class provides a method, prepareForSegue:sender:, which enables us to get a segue's identifier and destination view controller. Open CaptureViewController.m and override this method with the following implementation:

```
- (void)prepareForSegue:(UIStoryboardSegue *)segue
  sender:(id)sender {
  if ([segue.identifier isEqualToString:@"showReviewModally"]) {
    ReviewViewController *reviewViewController =
      segue.destinationViewController;
    Face mergedFace(faceToMerge0, faceToMerge1);
    reviewViewController.image = [self
      imageFromCapturedMat:mergedFace.getMat()];
  }
}
```

Note that we are using our Face constructor's merge version, which accepts two other Face objects as arguments.

To create a segue and assign its identifier, showReviewModally, let's reopen Main. storyboard. Right-click and drag from the **Merge** button to the view beneath **Review View Controller**, as shown in the following screenshot:

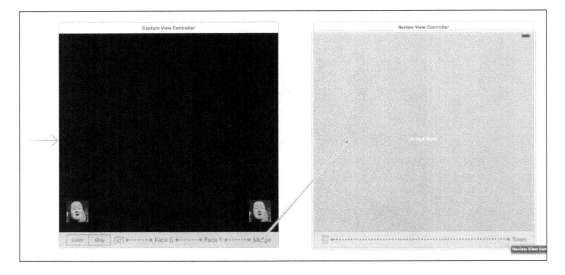

A dark context menu should appear. From the menu, select **Present Modally**, as shown in the following screenshot:

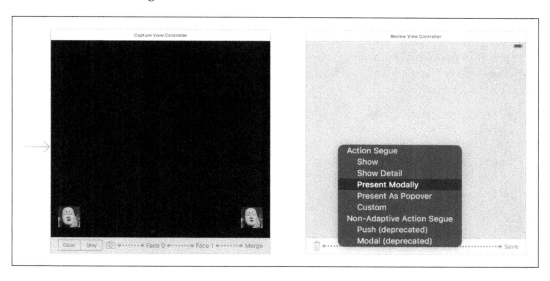

Now, in the scene hierarchy, **Capture View Controller Scene** should have a new child, **Present Modally segue to Review View Controller**. Select it. Open the inspector's **Attributes** pane (its icon looks like a slider). In the **Identifier** field, enter *showReviewModally*. From the **Transition** pull-down menu, select **Cross Dissolve** (or your favorite cheesy effect), as shown in the following screenshot:

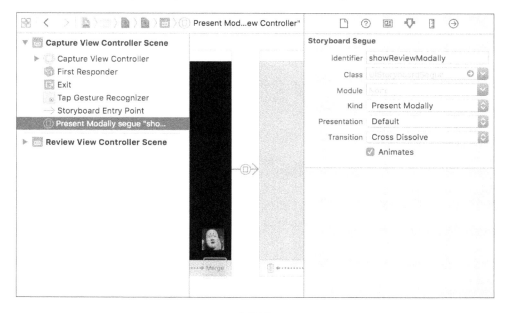

Detecting a hierarchy of face elements

As part of our face detection algorithm, we will reject cat faces that intersect with human faces. The reason is that the cat face cascade produces more false positives than the human face cascade. Thus, if a region is detected as both a human face and cat face, it is probably a human face in reality. To help us check for intersections between face rectangles, let's write a utility function, `intersects`. Declare the function in a new header file, `GeomUtils.h`, with the following code:

```
#ifndef GEOM_UTILS_H
#define GEOM_UTILS_H

#include <opencv2/core.hpp>

namespace GeomUtils {
  bool intersects(const cv::Rect &rect0, const cv::Rect &rect1);
}

#endif // !GEOM_UTILS_H
```

Two rectangles intersect if (and only if) a corner of one rectangle lies inside the other rectangle. Create another file, `GeomUtils.cpp`, with the following implementation of the `intersects` function in the file:

```
#include "GeomUtils.h"

bool GeomUtils::intersects(const cv::Rect &rect0,
  const cv::Rect &rect1)
{
  return
    rect0.x                 < rect1.x + rect1.width  &&
    rect0.x + rect0.width   > rect1.x                &&
    rect0.y                 < rect1.y + rect1.height &&
    rect0.y + rect0.height  > rect1.y;
}
```

Now, let's create a file, `FaceDetector.cpp`, for the implementation of the `FaceDetector` class. This file begins with the obvious import statements followed by a preprocessor macro that defines `EQUALIZE(src, dst)` as either a `cv::CLAHE::apply` method call or a simple `cv::equalizeHist` function call, depending on whether we set the `WITH_CLAHE` preprocessor flag. Here is the relevant code:

```
#include <opencv2/imgproc.hpp>

#include "FaceDetector.h"
```

```
#include "GeomUtils.h"

#ifdef WITH_CLAHE
#define EQUALIZE(src, dst) clahe->apply(src, dst)
#else
#define EQUALIZE(src, dst) cv::equalizeHist(src, dst)
#endif
```

Our face detection algorithm uses many constants. We will define them here, near the top of the file, where we can conveniently review and modify them. For the cascade classifiers, we will use the following kinds of constants:

- **Scale factor**: This ratio expresses the change in scale between the levels of the search. For example, if the scale factor is 1.4, a classifier might search for faces that are 140 x 140 pixels, then 100 x 100 pixels, and so on.

- **Minimum neighbors**: If this is greater than zero, the classifier merges this number of intersecting detection results in a neighborhood. If there are fewer intersections, the results in the neighborhood are rejected.

- **Minimum size**: This is the smallest scale that the classifier will search. We express the minimum face size as a proportion of the whole image size, and the minimum eye size as a proportion of the face size.

We will define different cascade classification constants for human faces, human eyes, and cat faces, as seen in the following code:

```
const double DETECT_HUMAN_FACE_SCALE_FACTOR = 1.4;
const int DETECT_HUMAN_FACE_MIN_NEIGHBORS = 4;
const int DETECT_HUMAN_FACE_RELATIVE_MIN_SIZE_IN_IMAGE = 0.25;

const double DETECT_HUMAN_EYE_SCALE_FACTOR = 1.2;
const int DETECT_HUMAN_EYE_MIN_NEIGHBORS = 2;
const int DETECT_HUMAN_EYE_RELATIVE_MIN_SIZE_IN_FACE = 0.1;

const double DETECT_CAT_FACE_SCALE_FACTOR = 1.4;
const int DETECT_CAT_FACE_MIN_NEIGHBORS = 6;
const int DETECT_CAT_FACE_RELATIVE_MIN_SIZE_IN_IMAGE = 0.2;
```

Some of the other constants represent the layout of eyes and noses in a typical face. We will express these layout values as a proportion of the face's or eye's width or height, and we will use different values for cats and humans. Here are the definitions:

```
const double ESTIMATE_HUMAN_EYE_CENTER_RELATIVE_X_IN_EYE = 0.5;
const double ESTIMATE_HUMAN_EYE_CENTER_RELATIVE_Y_IN_EYE = 0.65;

const double ESTIMATE_HUMAN_LEFT_EYE_CENTER_RELATIVE_X_IN_FACE =
    0.3;
const double ESTIMATE_HUMAN_RIGHT_EYE_CENTER_RELATIVE_X_IN_FACE =
    1.0 - ESTIMATE_HUMAN_LEFT_EYE_CENTER_RELATIVE_X_IN_FACE;
const double ESTIMATE_HUMAN_EYE_CENTER_RELATIVE_Y_IN_FACE = 0.4;

const double ESTIMATE_HUMAN_NOSE_RELATIVE_LENGTH_IN_FACE = 0.2;

const double ESTIMATE_CAT_LEFT_EYE_CENTER_RELATIVE_X_IN_FACE =
    0.25;
const double ESTIMATE_CAT_RIGHT_EYE_CENTER_RELATIVE_X_IN_FACE =
    1.0 - ESTIMATE_CAT_LEFT_EYE_CENTER_RELATIVE_X_IN_FACE;
const double ESTIMATE_CAT_EYE_CENTER_RELATIVE_Y_IN_FACE = 0.4;

const double ESTIMATE_CAT_NOSE_TIP_RELATIVE_X_IN_FACE = 0.5;
const double ESTIMATE_CAT_NOSE_TIP_RELATIVE_Y_IN_FACE = 0.75;
```

Finally, the following constants describe the BGR colors and radius that we use to draw rectangles and circles around the detected faces, eyes, and noses:

```
const cv::Scalar DRAW_HUMAN_FACE_COLOR(0, 255, 255); // Yellow
const cv::Scalar DRAW_CAT_FACE_COLOR(255, 255, 255); // White
const cv::Scalar DRAW_LEFT_EYE_COLOR(0, 0, 255); // Red
const cv::Scalar DRAW_RIGHT_EYE_COLOR(0, 255, 0); // Green
const cv::Scalar DRAW_NOSE_COLOR(255, 0, 0); // Blue

const int DRAW_RADIUS = 4;
```

Remember that a `FaceDetector`'s constructor accepts the paths to four cascade files. It initializes the corresponding cascade classifiers for a human face, cat face, human left eye, and human right eye. If the `WITH_CLAHE` preprocessor flag is set, the constructor also initializes a CLAHE algorithm. Here is the code:

```
FaceDetector::FaceDetector(
    const std::string &humanFaceCascadePath,
    const std::string &catFaceCascadePath,
    const std::string &humanLeftEyeCascadePath,
```

```
      const std::string &humanRightEyeCascadePath)
 : humanFaceClassifier(humanFaceCascadePath)
 , catFaceClassifier(catFaceCascadePath)
 , humanLeftEyeClassifier(humanLeftEyeCascadePath)
 , humanRightEyeClassifier(humanRightEyeCascadePath)
#ifdef WITH_CLAHE
 , clahe(cv::createCLAHE())
#endif
{
}
```

Now, let's consider the `detect` method's implementation. It is quite long, so we will look at it in three chunks. First, we clear any previous contents from the `vector<Face>` of results and we resize and equalize the image. The equalization is implemented in a helper method, `equalize`, which we will examine later. Here is the start of the `detect` method's implementation:

```
void FaceDetector::detect(cv::Mat &image,
  std::vector<Face> &faces, double resizeFactor, bool draw)
{
  faces.clear();

  if (resizeFactor == 1.0)
  {
    equalize(image);
  }
  else
  {
    cv::resize(image, resizedImage, cv::Size(), resizeFactor,
      resizeFactor, cv::INTER_AREA);
    equalize(resizedImage);
  }
```

Secondly, the method uses two of the cascade classifiers to find the rectangular bounds of human faces and cat faces in the resized, equalized image. As part of this step, we calculate the minimum face sizes in pixels, based on the constant proportions that we defined. The rectangles are stored in vectors, as seen in the following code:

```
  // Detect human faces.
  std::vector<cv::Rect> humanFaceRects;
  int detectHumanFaceMinWidth = MIN(image.cols, image.rows) *
    DETECT_HUMAN_FACE_RELATIVE_MIN_SIZE_IN_IMAGE;
  cv::Size detectHumanFaceMinSize(detectHumanFaceMinWidth,
    detectHumanFaceMinWidth);
```

```
humanFaceClassifier.detectMultiScale(equalizedImage,
  humanFaceRects, DETECT_HUMAN_FACE_SCALE_FACTOR,
  DETECT_HUMAN_FACE_MIN_NEIGHBORS, 0, detectHumanFaceMinSize);

// Detect cat faces.
std::vector<cv::Rect> catFaceRects;
int detectCatFaceMinWidth = MIN(image.cols, image.rows) *
  DETECT_CAT_FACE_RELATIVE_MIN_SIZE_IN_IMAGE;
cv::Size detectCatFaceMinSize(detectCatFaceMinWidth,
  detectCatFaceMinWidth);
catFaceClassifier.detectMultiScale(equalizedImage, catFaceRects,
  DETECT_CAT_FACE_SCALE_FACTOR, DETECT_CAT_FACE_MIN_NEIGHBORS,
  0, detectCatFaceMinSize);
```

Thirdly, we iterate over the rectangles, discard cat faces that intersect human faces, and pass the remaining items to the `detectInnerComponents` helper method. Each time we call the helper method, it constructs a `Face` object and adds it to the `vector<Face>` of results. Here are the relevant loops:

```
for (cv::Rect &humanFaceRect : humanFaceRects) {
  // Evaluate the human face.
  detectInnerComponents(image, faces, resizeFactor, draw, Human,
    humanFaceRect);

  // Discard cat faces that intersect the human face.
  // (The human face detector is more reliable.)
  catFaceRects.erase(std::remove_if(catFaceRects.begin(),
    catFaceRects.end(),
    [&humanFaceRect](cv::Rect &catFaceRect) {
      return GeomUtils::intersects(humanFaceRect, catFaceRect);
    }), catFaceRects.end());
}

for (cv::Rect &catFaceRect : catFaceRects) {
  // Evaluate the cat face.
  detectInnerComponents(image, faces, resizeFactor, draw, Cat,
    catFaceRect);
}
}
```

The `equalize` helper method performs grayscale conversion (if the image is not already grayscale) and applies either standard equalization or CLAHE, based on our `EQUALIZE` macro. Here is the method's implementation:

```
void FaceDetector::equalize(const cv::Mat &image)
{
  switch (image.channels()) {
    case 4:
      cv::cvtColor(image, equalizedImage, cv::COLOR_BGRA2GRAY);
      EQUALIZE(equalizedImage, equalizedImage);
      break;
    case 3:
      cv::cvtColor(image, equalizedImage, cv::COLOR_BGR2GRAY);
      EQUALIZE(equalizedImage, equalizedImage);
      break;
    default:
      // Assume the image is already grayscale.
      EQUALIZE(image, equalizedImage);
      break;
  }
}
```

The `detectInnerComponents` helper method is long, so we will consider it in eight chunks. (If this seems like a lot of chunks, just remember, it is only 2^3 or 1<<3.) First, we will define local variables that represent the face sub matrix and the eye and nose coordinates. The face sub-matrix has a reference to (not a copy of) the image data in the face region. Here is the start of `detectInnerComponents`:

```
void FaceDetector::detectInnerComponents(const cv::Mat &image,
    std::vector<Face> &faces, double resizeFactor, bool draw,
    Species species, cv::Rect faceRect)
{
  cv::Range rowRange(faceRect.y, faceRect.y + faceRect.height);
  cv::Range colRange(faceRect.x, faceRect.x + faceRect.width);

  bool isHuman = (species == Human);

  cv::Mat equalizedFaceMat(equalizedImage, rowRange, colRange);

  cv::Rect leftEyeRect;
  cv::Rect rightEyeRect;

  cv::Point2f leftEyeCenter;
  cv::Point2f rightEyeCenter;
  cv::Point2f noseTip;
```

If the face is human, we use a cascade classifier to search for the left eye in the left half of the face. If the classifier fails to detect the eye, we fall back to a naïve estimate of the eye's location in the face. Here is the relevant code:

```
if (isHuman) {
  int faceWidth = equalizedFaceMat.cols;
  int halfFaceWidth = faceWidth / 2;

  int eyeMinWidth = faceWidth *
    DETECT_HUMAN_EYE_RELATIVE_MIN_SIZE_IN_FACE;
  cv::Size eyeMinSize(eyeMinWidth, eyeMinWidth);

  // Try to detect the left eye.
  std::vector<cv::Rect> leftEyeRects;
  humanLeftEyeClassifier.detectMultiScale(
    equalizedFaceMat.colRange(0, halfFaceWidth),
    leftEyeRects, DETECT_HUMAN_EYE_SCALE_FACTOR,
    DETECT_HUMAN_EYE_MIN_NEIGHBORS, 0, eyeMinSize);
  if (leftEyeRects.size() > 0) {
    leftEyeRect = leftEyeRects[0];
    leftEyeCenter.x = leftEyeRect.x +
      ESTIMATE_HUMAN_EYE_CENTER_RELATIVE_X_IN_EYE *
      leftEyeRect.width;
    leftEyeCenter.y = leftEyeRect.y +
      ESTIMATE_HUMAN_EYE_CENTER_RELATIVE_Y_IN_EYE *
      leftEyeRect.height;
  } else {
    // Assume the left eye is in a typical location for a human.
    leftEyeCenter.x =
      ESTIMATE_HUMAN_LEFT_EYE_CENTER_RELATIVE_X_IN_FACE *
      faceRect.width;
    leftEyeCenter.y =
      ESTIMATE_HUMAN_EYE_CENTER_RELATIVE_Y_IN_FACE *
      faceRect.height;
  }
```

For the right eye, we follow the same approach, except that we search the right half of the face and use a different cascade classifier. We must adjust the detection result to be relative to the origin of the whole face, not the origin of the right half. Here is all the code to detect or naïvely estimate the right eye's coordinates:

```
  // Try to detect the right eye.
  std::vector<cv::Rect> rightEyeRects;
  humanRightEyeClassifier.detectMultiScale(
    equalizedFaceMat.colRange(halfFaceWidth, faceWidth),
    rightEyeRects, DETECT_HUMAN_EYE_SCALE_FACTOR,
```

```
                DETECT_HUMAN_EYE_MIN_NEIGHBORS, 0, eyeMinSize);
        if (rightEyeRects.size() > 0) {
          rightEyeRect = rightEyeRects[0];
          // Adjust the right eye rect to be relative to the whole
          // face.
          rightEyeRect.x += halfFaceWidth;
          rightEyeCenter.x = rightEyeRect.x +
            ESTIMATE_HUMAN_EYE_CENTER_RELATIVE_X_IN_EYE *
            rightEyeRect.width;
          rightEyeCenter.y = rightEyeRect.y +
            ESTIMATE_HUMAN_EYE_CENTER_RELATIVE_Y_IN_EYE *
            rightEyeRect.height;
        } else {
          // Assume the right eye is in a typical location for a
          // human.
          rightEyeCenter.x =
            ESTIMATE_HUMAN_RIGHT_EYE_CENTER_RELATIVE_X_IN_FACE *
            faceRect.width;
          rightEyeCenter.y =
            ESTIMATE_HUMAN_EYE_CENTER_RELATIVE_Y_IN_FACE *
            faceRect.height;
        }
```

As we do not have a cascade to detect a nose, we must make a naïve estimate about its coordinates. However, we can take advantage of the eye detection results, which may tell us that the face is tilted. If this is the case, the nose will be tilted too, and its tip will not be horizontally centered in the face rectangle. Instead, let's assume that if we find the line segment between the eyes, go to its midpoint, and then go down along a perpendicular line segment, we will reach the tip of the nose. This assumption is not perfect because it fails to account for perspective, yet it provides a useful adjustment for a slightly tilted face. Here is the relevant code:

```
        // Assume the nose is in a typical location for a human.
        // Consider the location of the eyes.
        cv::Point2f eyeDiff = rightEyeCenter - leftEyeCenter;
        cv::Point2f centerBetweenEyes = leftEyeCenter + 0.5 * eyeDiff;
        cv::Point2f noseNormal = cv::Point2f(-eyeDiff.y, eyeDiff.x) /
        sqrt(pow(eyeDiff.x, 2.0) + pow(eyeDiff.y, 2.0));
        double noseLength =
        ESTIMATE_HUMAN_NOSE_RELATIVE_LENGTH_IN_FACE *
        faceRect.height;
        noseTip = centerBetweenEyes + noseNormal * noseLength;
      }
```

For a cat, we do not have cascades to detect the eyes and nose. Thus, we always make naïve estimates about their coordinates, as seen in the following code:

```
else {
  // I haz kitteh! The face is a cat.
  // Assume the eyes and nose are in typical locations for a
  // cat.

  leftEyeCenter.x =
    ESTIMATE_CAT_LEFT_EYE_CENTER_RELATIVE_X_IN_FACE *
    faceRect.width;
  leftEyeCenter.y = ESTIMATE_CAT_EYE_CENTER_RELATIVE_Y_IN_FACE *
    faceRect.height;

  rightEyeCenter.x =
    ESTIMATE_CAT_RIGHT_EYE_CENTER_RELATIVE_X_IN_FACE *
    faceRect.width;
  rightEyeCenter.y =
    ESTIMATE_CAT_EYE_CENTER_RELATIVE_Y_IN_FACE *
    faceRect.height;

  noseTip.x = ESTIMATE_CAT_NOSE_TIP_RELATIVE_X_IN_FACE *
    faceRect.width;
  noseTip.y = ESTIMATE_CAT_NOSE_TIP_RELATIVE_Y_IN_FACE *
    faceRect.height;
}
```

At this stage, we have the eye and nose coordinates in the *resized* face sub-matrix. Let's restore the coordinates to the original scale, as seen in the following code:

```
// Restore everything to the original scale.

faceRect.x /= resizeFactor;
faceRect.y /= resizeFactor;
faceRect.width /= resizeFactor;
faceRect.height /= resizeFactor;

rowRange.start /= resizeFactor;
rowRange.end /= resizeFactor;

colRange.start /= resizeFactor;
colRange.end /= resizeFactor;

cv::Mat faceMat(image, rowRange, colRange);

leftEyeRect.x /= resizeFactor;
```

```
leftEyeRect.y /= resizeFactor;
leftEyeRect.width /= resizeFactor;
leftEyeRect.height /= resizeFactor;

rightEyeRect.x /= resizeFactor;
rightEyeRect.y /= resizeFactor;
rightEyeRect.width /= resizeFactor;
rightEyeRect.height /= resizeFactor;

leftEyeCenter /= resizeFactor;
rightEyeCenter /= resizeFactor;
noseTip /= resizeFactor;
```

Now, using a face sub-matrix at the original scale, let's create a new `Face` object and add it to the vector of results:

```
faces.push_back(Face(species, faceMat, leftEyeCenter,
rightEyeCenter, noseTip));
```

The `Face` constructor copies the sub-matrix, so now we may draw atop the original image without affecting `Face`. As the face sub-matrix has a different origin than the full image, we must adjust the eye and nose coordinates for the purpose of the drawing functions. Here is the relevant code, which completes the `detectInnerComponents` method:

```
if (draw) {
  cv::rectangle(image, faceRect.tl(), faceRect.br(),
    isHuman ? DRAW_HUMAN_FACE_COLOR : DRAW_CAT_FACE_COLOR);
  cv::circle(image, faceRect.tl() + cv::Point(leftEyeCenter),
    DRAW_RADIUS, DRAW_LEFT_EYE_COLOR);
  cv::circle(image, faceRect.tl() + cv::Point(rightEyeCenter),
    DRAW_RADIUS, DRAW_RIGHT_EYE_COLOR);
  cv::circle(image, faceRect.tl() + cv::Point(noseTip),
    DRAW_RADIUS, DRAW_NOSE_COLOR);

  if (leftEyeRect.width > 0) {
    cv::rectangle(image, faceRect.tl() + leftEyeRect.tl(),
      faceRect.tl() + leftEyeRect.br(), DRAW_LEFT_EYE_COLOR);
  }
  if (rightEyeRect.width > 0) {
    cv::rectangle(image, faceRect.tl() + rightEyeRect.tl(),
      faceRect.tl() + rightEyeRect.br(), DRAW_RIGHT_EYE_COLOR);
  }
}
```

Phew! That helper method really was long. I am reminded of a very old anecdote about a Scottish preacher who emigrated to Nova Scotia with his congregation. He prepared a series of sermons for the long sea voyage, and as the ship set sail from Aberdeen, he was building up to an interesting point: "Seventeenthly, friends, we encounter a great difficulty…"

 I am a Nova Scotian with Scots among my ancestors.

Aligning and blending face elements

The rest of our app's functionality is in the implementation of the Face class. Create a new file, Face.cpp. Remember that Face has a species, matrix of image data, and coordinates for the centers of the eyes and tip of the nose. Also remember that we designed Face as an immutable type, and for this reason the constructor copies a given matrix rather than storing a reference to external data. At the start of Face.cpp, let's implement the constructor that takes a species, matrix, and feature points as arguments:

```
#include <opencv2/imgproc.hpp>

#include "Face.h"

Face::Face(Species species, const cv::Mat &mat,
    const cv::Point2f &leftEyeCenter,
    const cv::Point2f &rightEyeCenter, const cv::Point2f &noseTip)
: species(species)
, leftEyeCenter(leftEyeCenter)
, rightEyeCenter(rightEyeCenter)
, noseTip(noseTip)
{
  mat.copyTo(this->mat);
}
```

Face also has the following default constructor for an empty face:

```
Face::Face() {
}
```

The following constructor copies the species, matrix, and feature points of another Face:

```
Face::Face(const Face &other)
: species(other.species)
, leftEyeCenter(other.leftEyeCenter)
, rightEyeCenter(other.rightEyeCenter)
, noseTip(other.noseTip)
{
  other.mat.copyTo(mat);
}
```

More interestingly, the Face class has another constructor to merge two given faces into a new face. This constructor checks the relative size of the given faces and passes them to a helper method with the signature, initMergedFace(const Face &biggerFace, const Face &smallerFace). Here is the constructor's code:

```
Face::Face(const Face &face0, const Face &face1) {
  if (face0.mat.total() > face1.mat.total()) {
    initMergedFace(face0, face1);
  } else {
    initMergedFace(face1, face0);
  }
}
```

Let's consider the helper method in four chunks. First, what is the species of the merged face? We shall say that two humans make a human, two cats make a cat, but a human and a cat make a hybrid. Therefore, the initMergedFace method starts like this:

```
void Face::initMergedFace(const Face &biggerFace,
  const Face &smallerFace)
{
  // Determine the species of the merged face.
  if (biggerFace.species == Human &&
      smallerFace.species == Human) {
    species = Human;
  } else if (biggerFace.species == Cat &&
      smallerFace.species == Cat) {
    species = Cat;
  } else {
    species = Hybrid;
  }
```

We want to warp the smaller face to map its eyes and nose to the same positions as the eyes and nose in the bigger face. This transformation can counteract many differences between the two faces, including differences in scale and rotation. OpenCV's `cv::getAffineTransformation` function can find the transformation matrix, and `cv::warpAffine` can apply it. Here is the relevant code:

```
// Warp the smaller face to align the eyes and nose with the
// bigger face.
cv::Point2f srcPoints[3] = {
  smallerFace.getLeftEyeCenter(),
  smallerFace.getRightEyeCenter(),
  smallerFace.getNoseTip()
};
cv::Point2f dstPoints[3] = {
  biggerFace.leftEyeCenter,
  biggerFace.rightEyeCenter,
  biggerFace.noseTip
};
cv::Mat affineTransform = cv::getAffineTransform(srcPoints,
  dstPoints);
cv::Size dstSize(biggerFace.mat.cols, biggerFace.mat.rows);
cv::warpAffine(smallerFace.mat, mat, affineTransform, dstSize);
```

Now, let's convert the warped image and original bigger face to the same color format (if they are not already in the same format). Then, we will blend them by multiplication. The resulting blend will be a bit darker than the input images, but it will be a pleasing effect because it will preserve dark or colorful facial features such as hair, fur, lips, freckles, irises, pupils, and the rims of eyeglasses. Here is the code for the color conversion and blending:

```
// Perform any necessary color conversion.
// Then, blend the warped face and the original bigger face.
switch (mat.channels() - biggerFace.mat.channels()) {
  case 3: {
    // The warped face is BGRA and the bigger face is grayscale.
    cv::Mat otherMat;
    cv::cvtColor(biggerFace.mat, otherMat, cv::COLOR_GRAY2BGRA);
    cv::multiply(mat, otherMat, mat, 1.0 / 255.0);
    break;
  }
  case 2: {
    // The warped face is BGR and the bigger face is grayscale.
    cv::Mat otherMat;
    cv::cvtColor(biggerFace.mat, otherMat, cv::COLOR_GRAY2BGR);
```

```
            cv::multiply(mat, otherMat, mat, 1.0 / 255.0);
            break;
        }
        case 1: {
            // The warped face is BGRA and the bigger face is BGR.
            cv::Mat otherMat;
            cv::cvtColor(biggerFace.mat, otherMat, cv::COLOR_BGR2BGRA);
            cv::multiply(mat, otherMat, mat, 1.0 / 255.0);
            break;
        }
        case -1:
            // The warped face is BGR and the bigger face is BGRA.
            cv::cvtColor(mat, mat, cv::COLOR_BGR2BGRA);
            cv::multiply(mat, biggerFace.mat, mat, 1.0 / 255.0);
            break;
        case -2:
            // The warped face is grayscale and the bigger face is BGR.
            cv::cvtColor(mat, mat, cv::COLOR_GRAY2BGR);
            cv::multiply(mat, biggerFace.mat, mat, 1.0 / 255.0);
            break;
        case -3:
            // The warped face is grayscale and the bigger face is BGRA.
            cv::cvtColor(mat, mat, cv::COLOR_GRAY2BGRA);
            cv::multiply(mat, biggerFace.mat, mat, 1.0 / 255.0);
            break;
        default:
            // The color formats are the same.
            cv::multiply(mat, biggerFace.mat, mat, 1.0 / 255.0);
            break;
    }
```

To finish the initialization of the merged face, let's copy the eye and nose coordinates from the original bigger face. By design, the warped and merged faces also have eyes and a nose at these coordinates. Here is the code to copy them:

```
    // The points of interest match the original bigger face.
    leftEyeCenter = biggerFace.leftEyeCenter;
    rightEyeCenter = biggerFace.rightEyeCenter;
    noseTip = biggerFace.noseTip;
}
```

Finally, for completeness, let's look at the one-line implementations of the `Face` class's getter methods. We define `isEmpty()` to be `true` if the `Face`'s matrix is empty, and this is the case for a `Face` constructed with the default constructor. Otherwise, the following code should be entirely self-explanatory:

```
bool Face::isEmpty() {
  return mat.empty();
}
Species Face::getSpecies() const {
  return species;
}
const cv::Mat &Face::getMat() const {
  return mat;
}
int Face::getWidth() const {
  return mat.cols;
}
int Face::getHeight() const {
  return mat.rows;
}
const cv::Point2f &Face::getLeftEyeCenter() const {
  return leftEyeCenter;
}
const cv::Point2f &Face::getRightEyeCenter() const {
  return rightEyeCenter;
}
const cv::Point2f &Face::getNoseTip() const {
  return noseTip;
}
```

That's all! The ManyMasks app is complete, with the ability to detect, preview, merge, save, and share faces.

Using the application and acting like a cat

Build ManyMasks and run it on an iOS device. For best results, obey the following guidelines:

- Work in an area with bright lighting and no shadows.
- Fill most of the frame with the face so that the image's resolution is not wasted on background areas.

- Capture an upright image of the face. This is especially important for a cat because our algorithm does not address the problem of locating the eyes and nose in a tilted cat face. To entice a cat to look straight at the camera, you might need to use a toy or treat.

- Capture a similar expression on the two faces. Like humans, cats have expressive faces, and different cats may develop different expressions as a form of communication with their humans. Here are some examples of my cats' expressions:

  - **Wide eyes:** Alert or assertive
  - **Narrow eyes:** Relaxed or submissive
  - **Yawn:** "Hello, my human."
  - **Meow:** "Pay attention, my human."
  - **Tongue between lips:** Paying attention to a scent, possibly a pleasant scent such as "my human". The tongue contributes to a cat's sense of smell.
  - **Licking nose:** "Feed me, my human."
  - **Curled lip, like Elvis Presley:** Disgust
  - **Compressed forehead:** Anger
  - **Hiss:** Rage
  - **Mouth hanging open:** Stress
  - **Quivering grin:** Hunting

Find a friend or a pet, and start blending faces! ManyMasks provides a fun exercise in portrait photography and acting.

Learning more about face analysis

Although our model of a face is a good start, we could make it much more sophisticated. We could model many feature points in order to accurately represent the differences between expressions, such as happiness and sadness. We could consider the third dimension and the camera's perspective. We could identify specific humans and specific cats based on the details of the face or even just the eye. We could train cascades for other species besides humans and cats.

Packt Publishing offers several more advanced OpenCV books with fascinating projects about face analysis. You can consider the following titles:

- *OpenCV 3 Blueprints* offers chapters on facial expression recognition, cascade training, and biometric identification of human faces, eyes, and fingerprints. The code is in C++.

- *OpenCV for Secret Agents* has a chapter on cascade training and biometric identification of human and cat faces. The code is in Python.

- *Mastering OpenCV with Practical Computer Vision Projects* provides chapters on face tracking with non-rigid features, 3D head tracking, and biometric identification of human faces, with code in C++.

Summary

This chapter has been a big step forward for us because we have focused on developing a modular and artificially intelligent solution. Unlike our previous apps, ManyMasks has multiple view controllers with a segue, as well as pure C++ classes dedicated to computer vision, and it is truly a smart application because it can classify things in its environment and perform computations based on their geometry. The next chapter will explore other smart approaches to problems of classification and geometry.

5
Classifying Coins and Commodities

Previously, in *Chapter 4, Detecting and Merging Faces of Mammals*, we used Haar or LBP cascades to classify the faces of humans and cats. We had a very specific classification problem because we wanted to blend faces, and conveniently, OpenCV provided pretrained cascade files for human and cat faces. Now, in our final chapter, we will tackle the broader problem of classifying a variety of objects without a ready-made classifier. Perhaps we could train a Haar or LBP cascade for each kind of object, but this would be a long project, requiring a lot of training images. Instead, we will develop a detector that requires no training and a classifier that requires only a few training images. Along the way, we will practice the following tasks:

1. Segment an image into foreground and background regions based on pixel colors. The result of the **segmentation** is a binary image called a **mask**. Each pixel in the mask is marked as either foreground (black) or background (white).

2. Make the mask smoother by expanding the foreground regions. This process is called **erosion**. It is a special case of **morphology**, which means morphing shapes' boundaries.

3. Detect the edges of the mask's foreground shapes or **blobs** and cropping out a rectangular image of each blob. This is a type of **contour analysis**.

4. Compare images of blobs based on a count of the colors in each image. This process is called **histogram analysis**.

5. Compare images of blobs based on scale-invariant and rotation-invariant descriptions of the textures in each image. This process is known as **feature matching** or **keypoint matching**.

You will configure the project with your own kinds of objects and your own training images. As examples, this chapter will discuss two kinds of dried beans and five kinds of Canadian coins, represented in the following set of training images:

Note that these training images vary in terms of scale and rotation. Our classifier will be scale-invariant and rotation-invariant. For each coin, we use two training images representing the obverse (heads) side and reverse (tails) side. From left to right and top to bottom, we have the following objects:

- **Pinto bean**: It is white with dark brown spots.

- **Romano bean**: It is brownish orange with dark brown spots.

- **Nickel (5-cent piece)**: It is nickel-plated. On the heads side, it shows Queen Elizabeth II. On the tails side, it shows a beaver.

- **Dime (10-cent piece)**: It is nickel-plated. On the heads side, it shows Queen Elizabeth II. On the tails side, it shows *The Bluenose*, a famous sailing ship from my province, Nova Scotia.

- **Quarter (25-cent piece)**: It is nickel-plated. On the heads side, it shows Queen Elizabeth II. On the tails side, it shows a caribou.

- **Loonie (dollar piece)**: It is brass-plated. On the heads side, it shows Queen Elizabeth II. On the tails side, it shows a loon.

- **Toonie (two-dollar piece)**: Its outer ring is nickel-plated and its inner circle is brass-plated. On the heads side, it shows Queen Elizabeth II. On the tails side, it shows a polar bear.

 The nickel, dime, and quarter have very similar designs on the heads side, so we expect some false classifications when we view these coins' heads.

Let's call our classification app BeanCounter, which is a colloquial term for an accountant or person who itemizes everything. By the end of the chapter, perhaps BeanCounter will inspire you to examine all the objects in your home or office and train a classifier for many of them!

 To obtain the completed projects for this book, you can refer to my GitHub repository at https://github.com/JoeHowse/iOSWithOpenCV or log in to your account on Packt Publishing's site at www.PacktPub.com. The project for *Chapter 5, Classifying Coins and Commodities*, is in the BeanCounter subfolder.

Understanding blob detection

A **blob** is a region that we can discern based on color. Perhaps the blob itself has a distinctive color, or perhaps the background does. Unlike the term "object", the term "blob" does not necessarily imply something with mass and volume. For example, surface variations such as stains can be blobs, even though they have negligible mass and volume. Optical effects can also be blobs. For example, a lens's aperture can produce **bokeh balls** or out-of-focus highlights that can make lights or shiny things appear strangely large and strangely similar to the aperture's shape. However, in BeanCounter, we tend to assume that a blob is a classifiable object.

The term "bokeh" comes from a Japanese word for bamboo. Different authors give different stories about the etymology, but perhaps someone thought bokeh balls resemble the bright rim of a chopped piece of bamboo.

Typically, a blob detector needs to solve the following sequence of problems:

1. **Segmentation**: Distinguish between the background colors and the foreground (blob) colors.

2. **Edge detection**: Distinguish between edge pixels and non-edge pixels. The **Canny** edge detection algorithm is a popular choice.

3. **Contour analysis**: Simplify the representation of the edges so that we may reason about them as geometric shapes.

Let's look at these steps one by one in the next few subsections.

Segmentation

This step is deceptively simple. We map a color range to the mask's background color (white) and the rest of the color ranges to the mask's foreground color (black), or vice versa. The `cv::inRange` function fits this purpose exactly. For some applications, we may *think* we know *a priori* what the correct color ranges will be. This is often a mistake. The lighting or the scene's contents may change unexpectedly, or we may just fail to consider a significant color.

Let's consider an example. When developers try to detect a human presence, they often rely on assumptions about the range of human skin colors, either in visible light or infrared light. These assumptions are often poorly tested, so the detector may have an unintended racial bias. Users have complained of such flaws in a wide range of computer vision devices, from Xbox Kinect to automatic soap dispensers.

Max Plenke of Tech.Mic has posted an interesting report on unintended racial bias in computer vision at http://mic.com/articles/124899/the-reason-this-racist-soap-dispenser-doesn-t-work-on-black-skin.

Rather than rely on rigid assumptions, we should consider an adaptive approach. We can choose a new background color range for each frame based on an analysis of the image. A simple and computationally cheap approach is to estimate the background range's center and width based on the mean color and standard deviation, respectively. The cv::meanStdDev function computes these statistics. More sophisticated approaches can use a history of multiple frames to build up a model of the background even as foreground objects move in and out. However, for BeanCounter's purposes, we will stay with the simpler approach.

The bgsegm module of opencv_contrib contains implementations of advanced segmentation techniques that use a history. See the official documentation at http://docs.opencv.org/3.1.0/d2/d55/group__bgsegm.html.

Canny edge detection

After generating a foreground mask, we want to detect the edges where the foreground and background meet. Previously, in my book, *OpenCV for Secret Agents* (Packt Publishing, 2015), I wrote the following description of edge detection in general, and the Canny algorithm specifically:

"[A] general approach to shape detection should start with an edge finding filter (marking edge regions as white and interior regions as black) and then a thresholding process. We define an edge as the discontinuity between neighboring regions of different brightness. Thus, an edge pixel has darker neighbors on one side and brighter neighbors on the opposite side. An edge-finding filter subtracts neighbor values from one side and adds them from the opposite side in order to measure how strongly a pixel exhibits this edge-like contrast in a given direction. To achieve a measurement that is independent of edges' direction, we can apply multiple filters (each oriented for edges of a different direction) and treat each filter's output as a dimension of a vector whose magnitude represents the overall "edginess" of the pixel. A set of such measurements for all pixels is sometimes called the **derivative** *of the image. Having computed the image's derivative, we select a threshold value based on the minimum contrast that we require in an edge. A high threshold accepts only high-contrast edges while a lower threshold also accepts lower-contrast edges.*

A popular edge-finding technique is the Canny algorithm. OpenCV's implementation, the [cv::Canny function in the imgproc module], performs both filtering and thresholding. As arguments, it takes a grayscale image, an output image, a low threshold value, and a high threshold value. The low threshold should accept all pixels that might be part of a good edge. The high threshold should accept only pixels that definitely are part of a good edge. From the set whose members might be edge pixels, the Canny algorithm accepts only the members that connect to definite edge pixels. The double criteria help to ensure that we can accept thin extremities of a major edge while rejecting edges that are altogether faint. For example, a pen stroke or the curb of a road extending into the distance can be a major edge with thin extremities."

 Note that the Canny edge-finding algorithm produces another mask, but this is an edge mask instead of a foreground mask. The edge mask is black in edge regions and white in non-edge regions.

Contour analysis

Given an edge mask, we can find sets of connected edge pixels by iteratively moving from one black pixel to an adjacent black pixel. This process is called **border following**. Then, we can approximate each set of edge pixels with a smaller number of points that define a contour. OpenCV implements this general approach in the cv::findContours function.

 Specifically, cv::findContours implements an algorithm that is described in the following paper:

Satoshi Suzuki. *Topological Structural Analysis of Digitized Binary Images by Border Following. Computer Vision, Graphics, and Image Processing*, Vol. 30 (1985), p. 32-46.

After finding a contour, we can simplify our model even further. We can find a simple geometric shape that approximates the contour's bounds. For this purpose, OpenCV provides functions such as cv::boundingRect and cv::boundingEllipse. A bounding rectangle is convenient because, in BeanCounter, we want to crop out a subimage of the blob.

For some applications, we may know *a priori* that we are only interested in blobs of a particular size or shape. Then, we can reject contours or bounding shapes that do not match our expectations. For BeanCounter, we reject very small blobs but we do not apply any other restrictions because we want to build a general-purpose detector.

Understanding histogram analysis

A **histogram** is a count of how many times each color occurs in an image. Typically, we do not count all possible colors separately; rather, we group similar colors together into bins. With a smaller number of bins, the histogram occupies less memory and offers a coarser basis of comparison. Typically, we want to choose some middle ground between very many bins (as the histograms tend to be highly dissimilar) and very few bins (as the histograms tend to be highly similar). For BeanCounter, let's start with 32 bins per channel (or 32^3=32678 bins in total), but you may change this value in the code to experiment with its effect.

A comparison of histograms can tell us whether two images contain similar colors. This kind of similarity alone does not necessarily mean that the images contain matching objects. For example, a silver fork and silver coin could have similar histograms. OpenCV supports several popular comparison algorithms. We will use the **Alternative Chi-Square** algorithm, which is a distance (dissimilarity) metric that heavily penalizes cases where a color is rare in one image but common in the other. Here is the algorithm in mathematical notation:

$$d(H_1, H_2) = 2 * \sum_I [(H_1(I) - H_2(I))_2 / (H_1(I) + H_2(I))]$$

Here is the equivalent pseudocode, which iterates over pairs of corresponding bins in two one-dimensional histograms:

```
function altChiSq(hist0, hist1):
  assert(hist0.length == hist1.length)
  dist = 0
  i = 0
  while i < hist0.length:
    dist += (hist0[i]-hist1[i])^2 / (hist0[i]+hist1[i])
    i += 1
  dist *= 2
  return dist
```

Multidimensional cases are similar, except that they involve multiple indices and nested loops.

 For a list of all OpenCV's histogram comparison algorithms and their formulae, see the official documentation at http://docs.opencv.org/3.1.0/d6/dc7/group__imgproc__hist.html#ga994f53817d621e2e4228fc646342d386.

OpenCV provides functions, `cv::calcHist` and `cv::compareHist`, to compute histograms and measure their similarity. OpenCV represents a histogram as a matrix with one dimension per color channel. For example, if we use all three channels in a BGR image, the histogram will have three dimensions.

 Note that in OpenCV, a multidimensional matrix is not the same as a multichannel matrix, and many OpenCV functions cannot handle matrices with more than two dimensions.

Understanding keypoint matching

Previously, in the *Understanding detection with cascade classifiers* section in *Chapter 4, Detecting and Merging Faces of Mammals*, we considered the problem of searching for a set of high-contrast features at various positions and various levels of magnification or scale. As we saw, Haar and LBP cascade classifiers solve this problem. Thus, we may say they are **scale-invariant** (robust to changes in scale). However, we also noted that these solutions are not **rotation-invariant** (robust to changes in rotation). Why? Consider the individual features. Haar-like features include edges, lines, and dots, which are all symmetric. LBP features are gradients, which may be symmetric, too. A symmetric feature cannot give us a clear indication of the object's rotation.

Now, let's consider solutions that are both scale-invariant and rotation-invariant. They must use asymmetric features called **corners**. A corner has brighter neighbors across one range of directions and darker neighbors across the remaining range of directions. One range must be bigger than the other, or else the feature is an edge, not a corner. For example, a reference image of an object might contain a right-angle corner with brighter neighbors ranging from the 12 o'clock to 3 o'clock directions and darker neighbors ranging from the 3 o'clock to 12 o'clock directions. If we find that a scene contains a right-angle corner with brighter neighbors ranging from the 1 o'clock to 4 o'clock directions, we may perhaps match this feature (along with others) to the reference. Then, we can infer that the scene's object is rotated 30 degrees clockwise relative to the reference object. Broadly, this type of scale- and rotation-invariant comparison has three steps:

1. **Detect** corners.
2. **Extract** descriptors, which are statistics about each corner.
3. **Match** descriptors from different images.

Often, detection and extraction are part of one algorithm, but the matcher is another algorithm that can work with many kinds of descriptors. Let's consider two popular pairs of algorithms: the SURF detector/extractor with the FLANN matcher and the ORB detector/extractor with the brute-force matcher.

OpenCV's official documentation contains an excellent set of tutorials on all the supported detection, extraction, and matching algorithms. Visit `http://docs.opencv.org/3.1.0/db/d27/tutorial_py_table_of_contents_feature2d.html`.

For more great tutorials on extraction, see Gil Levi's blog posts on the topic, starting with his A Short introduction to descriptors at `https://gilscvblog.wordpress.com/2013/08/18/a-short-introduction-to-descriptors/`.

SURF and FLANN

One approach to corner detection is to find the difference between the image's original version and a blurred version. This difference will be largest at corners. An algorithm called **Scale-Invariant Feature Transform** (**SIFT**) popularized this approach. For each detected corner, SIFT extracts a descriptor that includes 128 grayscale histogram bins for various brightness levels and various regions surrounding the corner. A newer algorithm, **Speeded-up Robust Features** (**SURF**), follows the same general approach as SIFT but applies many optimizations.

SIFT and SURF are patented, so I recommend that you only use them for non-commercial research purposes or study. They are implemented in the `cv::xfeatures2d::SIFT` and `cv::xfeatures2d::SURF` classes of the xfeatures2d module of `opencv_contrib`. These are subclasses of `cv::Feature2D`, which is part of the standard features module.

For SIFT and SURF, a popular matcher is **Fast Library for Approximate Nearest Neighbors** (**FLANN**). FLANN is optimized for nearest-neighbor searches in large datasets with high-dimensional spaces, such as the SIFT or SURF descriptors with 128 elements. The `cv::DescriptorMatcher` class implements many algorithms including FLANN, and we choose the algorithm via a factory function, `cv::DescriptorMatcher::create`. The `cv::DescriptorMatcher` class is part of the standard features2d module, and the FLANN implementation depends on the standard FLANN module.

If `opencv_contrib` is available, BeanCounter will use SURF and FLANN. This combination offers acceptable speed and good reliability and is widely used in industry despite the SURF patent.

ORB and brute-force Hamming-distance matching

Compared to SIFT and SURF, several other algorithms offer the advantages of being free, using less memory, and running faster, though they are less reliable.

Features from Accelerated Segment Test (FAST) is a corner detection algorithm that does not rely on a blur filter. It just considers differences in brightness within neighboring pixels and quickly rejects a neighborhood if the first few pixels do not look like a corner. FAST is not rotation-invariant.

Binary Robust Independent Elementary Features (BRIEF) is a descriptor extraction algorithm that produces a vector of binary elements (0 or 1). Each element represents the relative brightness of a pair of regions surrounding the corner. A value of 1 indicates that the first region is brighter. BRIEF is not rotation-invariant.

Oriented FAST and Rotated BRIEF (ORB) uses a variant of FAST for detection and a BRIEF variant for extraction. ORB is faster than the original FAST and BRIEF, and unlike them, it is rotation-invariant.

For details of the ORB algorithm, see the following paper, written by some of OpenCV's developers:

Ethan Rublee, Vincent Rabaud, Kurt Konolige, and Gary Bradski. *ORB: an efficient alternative to SIFT or SURF*. Menlo Park, California: Willow Garage, 2011. http://www.willowgarage.com/sites/default/files/orb_final.pdf

FAST, BRIEF, and ORB are implemented in the `cv::FastFeatureDetector`, `cv::xfeatures2d::BriefDescriptorExtractor`, and `cv::ORB` classes. These are subclasses of `cv::Feature2D`.

For BRIEF, ORB, and other binary descriptors, it is appropriate to use brute-force matching with the Hamming distance as the metric. **Brute-force matching** simply consists of choosing matches that minimize a metric of distance between the pairs of matched descriptor vectors. The **Hamming distance** is a count of the vector elements that differ. The `cv::DescriptorMatcher` class implements many algorithms including brute-force Hamming distance, and we choose the algorithm via a factory function, `cv::DescriptorMatcher::create`.

If `opencv_contrib` is unavailable, BeanCounter will use ORB and brute-force matching. This combination offers good speed and acceptable reliability. It is widely used, especially for mobile and embedded applications.

Planning an object classification application

At startup, BeanCounter loads a configuration file and set of images and trains the classifier. This may take several seconds. While loading, the app displays the text **Training classifier...**, along with a regal image of Queen Elizabeth II and eight dried beans:

Next, BeanCounter shows a live view from the rear-facing camera. A blob detection algorithm is applied to each frame and a green rectangle is drawn around each detected blob. Consider the following screenshot:

Note the controls in the toolbar below the camera view. The **Image** and **Mask** segmented controls enable the user to toggle between the preceding view of detection results in the image and the following view of the mask:

 The gray dots in the preceding image are just an artifact of the iOS screenshot function, which sometimes shows a faint ghost of a previous frame. The mask is really pure black and pure white.

The switch camera button has the usual effect of activating a different camera (front-facing or rear-facing).

When the user presses the **Classify** button, BeanCounter classifies the image of the blob. This process may take a few seconds. When the result is ready, the app shows a large view of the blob with a caption that describes the classification. Refer to the following screenshot:

Again, note the toolbar items. The trash and **Save** buttons have the same behavior as they did in our previous applications, LightWork and ManyMasks. Once again, if the user saves an image, the app prompts the user to share it via social media (or not). When the user has finished reviewing the classification result and trashed or saved the image, BeanCounter returns to its capture and detection mode.

Configuring the project

Create an Xcode project named BeanCounter. As usual, choose the **Single View Application** template. Follow the configuration instructions in *Chapter 1, Setting Up Software and Hardware* and *Chapter 2, Capturing, Storing, and Sharing Photos*. (See the *Configuring the project* section of each chapter.) BeanCounter depends on the same frameworks and device capabilities as LightWork.

Our blob classifier will depend on a configuration file and set of training images that we provide. As a starting point, you may want to use the training set of beans and Canadian coins, as provided in the book's GitHub repository. Alternatively, under the Supporting Files folder, add your own training images and create a new file called BlobClassifierTraining.plist. Edit the PLIST file to define labels and training images according to the format in the following screenshot:

Key	Type	Value
▼ Root	Dictionary	(2 items)
▼ labelDescriptions	Array	(9 items)
Item 0	String	unidentified
Item 1	String	Canadian penny
Item 2	String	Canadian nickel
Item 3	String	Canadian dime
Item 4	String	Canadian quarter
Item 5	String	loonie, Canadian dollar
Item 6	String	toonie, Canadian two-dollar
Item 7	String	pinto bean
Item 8	String	romano bean
▼ blobs	Array	(12 items)
▼ Item 0	Dictionary	(2 items)
imageFilename	String	CanadianNickel_Heads_000.png
label	Number	2
▶ Item 1	Dictionary	(2 items)
▶ Item 2	Dictionary	(2 items)
▶ Item 3	Dictionary	(2 items)
▶ Item 4	Dictionary	(2 items)
▶ Item 5	Dictionary	(2 items)
▶ Item 6	Dictionary	(2 items)
▶ Item 7	Dictionary	(2 items)
▶ Item 8	Dictionary	(2 items)
▶ Item 9	Dictionary	(2 items)
▶ Item 10	Dictionary	(2 items)
▶ Item 11	Dictionary	(2 items)

For example, **Item 0** in **blobs** is a training image with the filename CanadianNickel_ Heads_000.png and the label 2. We can look up the 2 label's description in **labelDescriptions**, where **Item 2** is Canadian nickel. Thus, CanadianNickel_ Heads_000.png is a training image for Canadian nickel.

Later, in the *Capturing and previewing blobs* section, we will parse this configuration file and use its values. **Item 0** in **labelDescriptions** should describe an unknown or unclassified object, but otherwise you are free to choose any labels and training images.

If you use a large training set, you may run into problems with slow startup, slow classification, and memory shortages. Typically, large-scale classification systems rely on remote servers where processing power and memory are relatively plentiful. BeanCounter uses a simple approach that works for a small-scale classification system on a disconnected mobile device.

After completing the PLIST file, select **BeanCounter** in the project navigator pane. Open the **Build Phases** tab in the editor area and make sure that BlobClassifierTraining.plist and the training images appear in the **Copy Bundle Resources** list.

Defining blobs and a blob detector

For our purposes, a blob simply has an image and label. The image is cv::Mat and the label is an unsigned integer. The label's default value is 0, which shall signify that the blob has not yet been classified. Create a new header file, Blob.h, and fill it with the following declaration of a Blob class:

```
#ifndef BLOB_H
#define BLOB_H

#include <opencv2/core.hpp>

class Blob
{
public:
  Blob(const cv::Mat &mat, uint32_t label = 0ul);

  /**
   * Construct an empty blob.
   */
```

```
    Blob();

    /**
     * Construct a blob by copying another blob.
     */
    Blob(const Blob &other);

    bool isEmpty() const;

    uint32_t getLabel() const;
    void setLabel(uint32_t value);

    const cv::Mat &getMat() const;
    int getWidth() const;
    int getHeight() const;

private:
    uint32_t label;

    cv::Mat mat;
};


#endif // BLOB_H
```

The image of `Blob` does not change after construction, but the label may change as a result of our classification process. Note that most of the methods of `Blob` have the `const` modifier, but of course, `setLabel` does not because it changes the label.

Now, let's declare a `BlobDetector` class in another new header file, `BlobDetector.h`. This class provides a `detect` public method to analyze a given image and populate a `vector<Blob>` based on detected objects in the image. Another public method, `getMask`, returns a thresholded version of the most recent image that the `detect` method received. Internally, `BlobDetector` uses several more matrices and vectors to hold intermediate results, including the mask, detected edges, detected contours, and hierarchy that describes the contours' relationship to each other. Here is the detector's declaration:

```
class BlobDetector
{
public:
    void detect(cv::Mat &image, std::vector<Blob> &blob,
```

```
        double resizeFactor = 1.0, bool draw = false);

    const cv::Mat &getMask() const;

private:
    void createMask(const cv::Mat &image);

    cv::Mat resizedImage;
    cv::Mat mask;
    cv::Mat edges;
    std::vector<std::vector<cv::Point>> contours;
    std::vector<cv::Vec4i> hierarchy;
};


#endif // !BLOB_DETECTOR_H
```

Later, in the *Detecting blobs against a plain background* section, we will define the methods' bodies in new files called `Blob.cpp` and `BlobDetector.cpp`.

Defining blob descriptors and a blob classifier

Earlier in this chapter, in the *Understanding keypoint matching* section, we introduced the concept that a keypoint has a descriptor or set of descriptive statistics. Similarly, we can define a custom descriptor for a blob. As our classifier relies on histogram comparison and keypoint matching, let's say that a blob's descriptor consists of a normalized histogram and a matrix of keypoint descriptors. The descriptor object is also a convenient place to put the label. Create a new header file, `BlobDescriptor.h`, and put the following declaration of a `BlobDescriptor` class in it:

```
#ifndef BLOB_DESCRIPTOR_H
#define BLOB_DESCRIPTOR_H

#include <opencv2/core.hpp>

class BlobDescriptor
{
public:
    BlobDescriptor(const cv::Mat &normalizedHistogram,
        const cv::Mat &keypointDescriptors, uint32_t label);

    const cv::Mat &getNormalizedHistogram() const;
```

```
    const cv::Mat &getKeypointDescriptors() const;
    uint32_t getLabel() const;

private:
  cv::Mat normalizedHistogram;
  cv::Mat keypointDescriptors;
  uint32_t label;
};


  #endif // !BLOB_DESCRIPTOR_H
```

Note that `BlobDescriptor` is designed as an immutable class. All its methods, except the constructor, have the `const` modifier.

Now, let's declare a `BlobClassifier` class in another new header file, `BlobClassifier.h`. Publicly, this class receives `Blob` objects via an `update` method (for reference blobs) and a `classify` method (for blobs that the detector found in the scene). Privately, `BlobClassifier` creates, owns, and compares `BlobDescriptor` objects that pertain to the `Blob` objects. Thus, `BlobClassifier` is the only part of our program that needs to deal with `BlobDescriptor`. `BlobClassifier` also owns instances of OpenCV classes that are responsible for keypoint detection, description, and matching. Here is our classifier's declaration:

```
  #ifndef BLOB_CLASSIFIER_H
  #define BLOB_CLASSIFIER_H

  #import "Blob.h"
  #import "BlobDescriptor.h"

  #include <opencv2/features2d.hpp>

  class BlobClassifier
  {
  public:
    BlobClassifier();

    /**
     * Add a reference blob to the classification model.
     */
    void update(const Blob &referenceBlob);

    /**
     * Clear the classification model.
     */
```

```
    void clear();

    /**
     * Classify a blob that was detected in a scene.
     */
    void classify(Blob &detectedBlob) const;

private:
    BlobDescriptor createBlobDescriptor(const Blob &blob) const;
    float findDistance(const BlobDescriptor &detectedBlobDescriptor,
      const BlobDescriptor &referenceBlobDescriptor) const;

    /**
     * An adaptive equalizer to enhance local contrast.
     */
    cv::Ptr<cv::CLAHE> clahe;

    /**
     * A feature detector and descriptor extractor.
     * It finds features in images.
     * Then, it creates descriptors of the features.
     */
    cv::Ptr<cv::Feature2D> featureDetectorAndDescriptorExtractor;

    /**
     * A descriptor matcher.
     * It matches features based on their descriptors.
     */
    cv::Ptr<cv::DescriptorMatcher> descriptorMatcher;

    /**
     * Descriptors of the reference blobs.
     */
    std::vector<BlobDescriptor> referenceBlobDescriptors;
};

#endif // !BLOB_CLASSIFIER_H
```

Later, in the *Classifying blobs by color and keypoints* section, we will write the methods'
bodies in new files called `BlobDescriptor.cpp` and `BlobClassifier.cpp`.

Laying out the splash screen

`LaunchScreen.storyboard` defines the splash screen's layout, including the background image and the **Training classifier...** label. Refer to the following screenshot as a layout guide (or just download the completed storyboard from the book's GitHub repository):

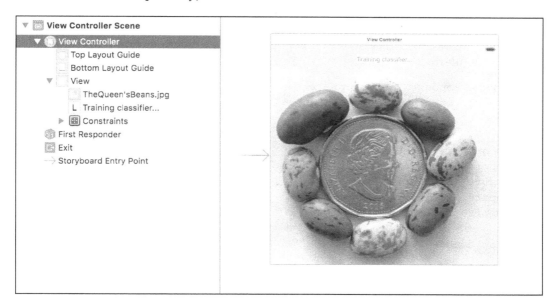

Defining and laying out the view controllers

BeanCounter uses two view controllers. The first enables the user to capture and preview images of blobs. The second enables the user to review a blob's classification result and save and share the image of the blob. A segue enables the first view controller to instantiate the second and pass a blob and label to it. This is similar to how we divided the application logic in the project, ManyMasks, in *Chapter 4, Detecting and Merging Faces of Mammals*, so we are able to reuse some code.

Capturing and previewing blobs

Import copies of the `VideoCamera.h` and `VideoCamera.m` files that we created in *Chapter 2, Capturing, Storing, and Sharing Photos*. These files contain our `VideoCamera` class, which extends OpenCV's `CvVideoCamera` to fix bugs and add new functionality.

Also import copies of the `CaptureViewController.h` and
`CaptureViewController.m` files that we created in *Chapter 4, Detecting and
Merging Faces of Mammals*. These files contain our `CaptureViewController`
class, which is responsible for capture and detection. Of course, our new version
of `CaptureViewController` does not depend on our old model of faces and a
face detector. Instead, it depends on our new model of blobs, a blob detector,
and a blob classifier. The new version also keeps a list of strings describing
the possible classification labels. The user interface has changed a bit, too. Edit
`CaptureViewController.m` so that it begins with the following import statements
and private interface:

```objc
#import <opencv2/core.hpp>
#import <opencv2/imgcodecs/ios.h>
#import <opencv2/imgproc.hpp>

#import "CaptureViewController.h"
#import "BlobClassifier.h"
#import "BlobDetector.h"
#import "ReviewViewController.h"
#import "VideoCamera.h"

const double DETECT_RESIZE_FACTOR = 0.5;

@interface CaptureViewController () <CvVideoCameraDelegate> {
  BlobClassifier *blobClassifier;
  BlobDetector *blobDetector;
  std::vector<Blob> detectedBlobs;
}

@property IBOutlet UIView *backgroundView;
@property IBOutlet UIBarButtonItem *classifyButton;

@property VideoCamera *videoCamera;
@property BOOL showMask;

@property NSArray<NSString *> *labelDescriptions;

- (IBAction)onTapToSetPointOfInterest:
    (UITapGestureRecognizer *)tapGesture;
- (IBAction)onPreviewModeSelected:
    (UISegmentedControl *)segmentedControl;
- (IBAction)onSwitchCameraButtonPressed;

- (void)refresh;
```

```
- (void)processImage:(cv::Mat &)mat;
- (UIImage *)imageFromCapturedMat:(const cv::Mat &)mat;

@end
```

Our `viewDidLoad` method is responsible for initializing the detector, classifier, list of label descriptions, and camera. As part of this process, we load metadata about our classifier's training set from `BlobClassiferTraining.plist`. (For a description of this PLIST file, refer back to the *Configuring the project* section earlier in this chapter.) The iOS SDK makes it easy for us to load PLIST as a dictionary of key-value pairs. The keys are strings and the values may be other dictionaries, arrays, strings, numbers, Booleans, dates, or raw binary data. For BeanCounter's purposes, the PLIST file provides label descriptions as well as pairs of training images and their labels. We load each image from file, construct `Blob` with the image and its label, and pass `Blob` to the `update` method of `BlobClassifier` to train the classifier. See the highlighted code in the following implementation of `viewDidLoad`:

```
@implementation CaptureViewController

- (void)viewDidLoad {
  [super viewDidLoad];

  blobDetector = new BlobDetector();
  blobClassifier = new BlobClassifier();

  // Load the blob classifier's configuration from file.
  NSBundle *bundle = [NSBundle mainBundle];
  NSString *configPath = [bundle
    pathForResource:@"BlobClassifierTraining"
    ofType:@"plist"];
  NSDictionary *config = [NSDictionary
    dictionaryWithContentsOfFile:configPath];

  // Remember the descriptions of the blob labels.
  self.labelDescriptions = config[@"labelDescriptions"];

  // Create reference blobs and train the blob classifier.
  NSArray *configBlobs = config[@"blobs"];
  for (NSDictionary *configBlob in configBlobs) {
    uint32_t label = [configBlob[@"label"] unsignedIntValue];
    NSString *imageFilename = configBlob[@"imageFilename"];
    UIImage *image = [UIImage imageNamed:imageFilename];
    if (image == nil) {
      NSLog(@"Image not found in resources: %@", imageFilename);
```

```
      continue;
    }
    cv::Mat mat;
    UIImageToMat(image, mat);
    cv::cvtColor(mat, mat, cv::COLOR_RGB2BGR);
    Blob blob(mat, label);
    blobClassifier->update(blob);
  }

  self.videoCamera = [[VideoCamera alloc]
    initWithParentView:self.backgroundView];
  self.videoCamera.delegate = self;
  self.videoCamera.defaultAVCaptureSessionPreset =
    AVCaptureSessionPresetHigh;
  self.videoCamera.defaultFPS = 30;
  self.videoCamera.letterboxPreview = YES;
  self.videoCamera.defaultAVCaptureDevicePosition =
    AVCaptureDevicePositionBack;
}
```

The `BlobClassifier` and `BlobDetector` are dynamically allocated C++ objects. The classifier uses a lot of memory because it holds the histograms and keypoint descriptors of all the reference images. Let's edit the `didReceiveMemoryWarning` and `dealloc` methods to ensure that these C++ objects get cleaned up:

```
- (void)didReceiveMemoryWarning {
  [super didReceiveMemoryWarning];

  if (blobClassifier != NULL) {
    delete blobClassifier;
    blobClassifier = NULL;
  }
  if (blobDetector != NULL) {
    delete blobDetector;
    blobDetector = NULL;
  }
}

- (void)dealloc {
  if (blobClassifier != NULL) {
    delete blobClassifier;
    blobClassifier = NULL;
  }
  if (blobDetector != NULL) {
```

```
    delete blobDetector;
    blobDetector = NULL;
  }
}
```

When the user selects an option in the **Image** and **Mask** segmented controls, we set the `showMask` Boolean property, as shown in the following code:

```
- (IBAction)onPreviewModeSelected:
    (UISegmentedControl *)segmentedControl {
  switch (segmentedControl.selectedSegmentIndex) {
    case 0:
      self.showMask = NO;
      break;
    default:
      self.showMask = YES;
      break;
  }
  [self refresh];
}
```

Now, let's consider how BeanCounter handles each frame of camera input. The `processImage:` callback begins with our usual code to correct the orientation. Then, we pass the frame and `vector<Blob>` to the `detect` method of `BlobDetector`, which populates the vector and draws green rectangles around detected blobs in the image. We enable or disable the **Classify** button, depending on whether any blobs were detected. If the `showMask` property is `true`, we show the mask by copying it to the current frame. Otherwise, the user will see the image with green rectangles around the blobs. Here is the callback's implementation:

```
- (void)processImage:(cv::Mat &)mat {

  switch (self.videoCamera.defaultAVCaptureVideoOrientation) {
    case AVCaptureVideoOrientationLandscapeLeft:
    case AVCaptureVideoOrientationLandscapeRight:
      // The landscape video is captured upside-down.
      // Rotate it by 180 degrees.
      cv::flip(mat, mat, -1);
      break;
    default:
      break;
  }

  // Detect and draw any blobs.
```

```
blobDetector->detect(mat, detectedBlobs, DETECT_RESIZE_FACTOR,
  true);

BOOL didDetectBlobs = (detectedBlobs.size() > 0);
dispatch_async(dispatch_get_main_queue(), ^{
  self.classifyButton.enabled = didDetectBlobs;
});

if (self.showMask) {
  blobDetector->getMask().copyTo(mat);
}
}
```

The rest of the methods of `CaptureViewController` have the same implementations as they did in the project, ManyMasks, in *Chapter 4, Detecting and Merging Faces of Mammals*.

Open `Main.storyboard` and select **ViewController** in the scene hierarchy. Open the inspector's **Identity** tab and change **Class** to **CaptureViewController**. Now, add the appropriate GUI widgets as children of the view controller's main view. Refer to the following screenshot as a layout guide (or just download the completed storyboard from the book's GitHub repository):

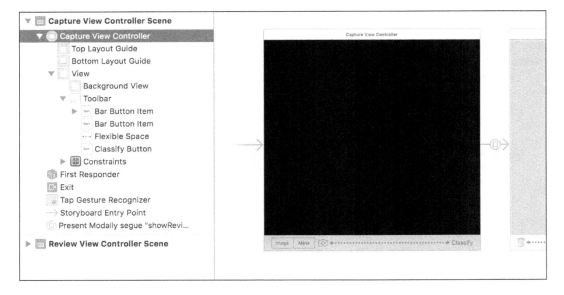

Right-click on **Capture View Controller** in the scene hierarchy to see the list of available outlets and actions, which we defined in `CaptureViewController.m`. Set the connections so that they match the following screenshot:

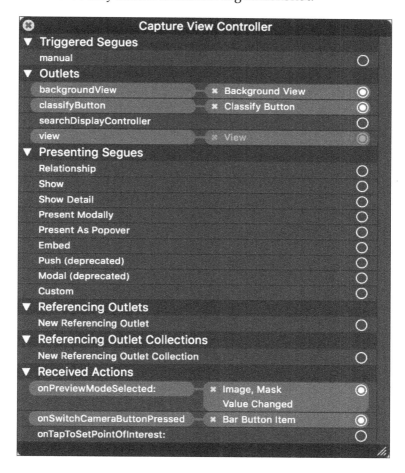

Reviewing, saving, and sharing classified blobs

Add copies of the `ReviewViewController.h` and `ReviewViewController.m` files from the project, ManyMasks, in *Chapter 4, Detecting and Merging Faces of Mammals*. For BeanCounter's purposes, we will edit these files to support a caption, which will describe the classification result. First, edit the public interface in `ReviewViewController.h` to add an `NSString` property, as seen in the following code:

```
@interface ReviewViewController : UIViewController

@property UIImage *image;
@property NSString *caption;

@end
```

Edit the private interface in `ReviewViewController.m` to add a `UILabel` property, as indicated in the following code excerpt:

```
@interface ReviewViewController ()

@property IBOutlet UIImageView *imageView;
@property IBOutlet UILabel *label;
@property IBOutlet UIActivityIndicatorView *activityIndicatorView;
@property IBOutlet UIToolbar *toolbar;

// ... same methods as in Chapter 4 ...

@end
```

Finally, edit the implementation of the `viewDidLoad` method to assign the caption as the label's text:

```
- (void)viewDidLoad {
  [super viewDidLoad];

  self.imageView.image = self.image;
  self.label.text = self.caption;
}
```

The rest of the `ReviewViewController` class remains unchanged. Notably, the class still supports saving and sharing the image.

Let's open `Main.storyboard`. Drag a new view controller from the library pane to the editor area. Open the new view controller's **Identity** inspector and set **Class** to **ReviewViewController**. Now, add the appropriate GUI widgets as children of the view controller's main view. Refer to the following screenshot as a layout guide (or just download the completed storyboard from the book's GitHub repository):

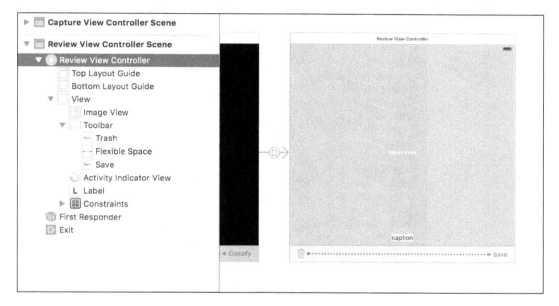

Right-click on **Review View Controller** in the scene hierarchy to see the list of available outlets and actions, which we defined in `ReviewViewController.m`. Set the connections so that they match the following screenshot:

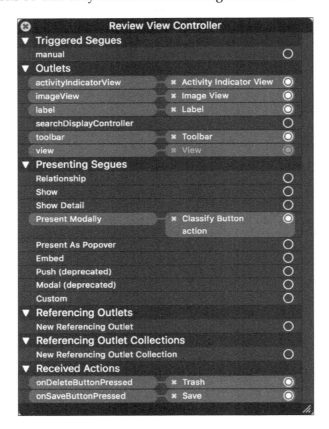

Seguing between the view controllers

Let's examine the `prepareForSegue` method where our `CaptureViewController` provides a blob and classification result to the `ReviewViewController`. First, the method stops the video camera because we do not want the `processImage:` method to change the vector of blobs on another thread while we are accessing the blobs here. Then, `prepareForSegue` chooses the biggest blob and passes it to the `classify` method of `BlobClassifier`, which returns a classification label as an integer. We look up the label's description, and then finally provide the blob's image and label's description to the `ReviewViewController`. Here is the relevant code:

```
- (void)prepareForSegue:
    (UIStoryboardSegue *)segue sender:(id)sender {
```

```
if ([segue.identifier isEqualToString:@"showReviewModally"]) {
  ReviewViewController *reviewViewController =
    segue.destinationViewController;

  // Stop the camera to prevent conflicting access to the blobs.
  [self.videoCamera stop];

  // Find the biggest blob.
  int biggestBlobIndex = 0;
  for (int i = 0, biggestBlobArea = 0;
      i < detectedBlobs.size(); i++) {
    Blob &detectedBlob = detectedBlobs[i];
    int blobArea = detectedBlob.getWidth() *
      detectedBlob.getHeight();
    if (blobArea > biggestBlobArea) {
      biggestBlobIndex = i;
      biggestBlobArea = blobArea;
    }
  }
  Blob &biggestBlob = detectedBlobs[biggestBlobIndex];

  // Classify the blob and show the result in the destination
  // view controller.
  blobClassifier->classify(biggestBlob);
  reviewViewController.image = [self
    imageFromCapturedMat:biggestBlob.getMat()];
  reviewViewController.caption =
    self.labelDescriptions[biggestBlob.getLabel()];
  }
}
```

Reopen `Main.storyboard` and create a segue by right-clicking and dragging from the **Classify** button to **Review View Controller**. The segue's **Kind** should be **Present Modally**, its **Identifier** should be **showReviewModally**, and its **Transition** should be **Flip Horizontal** (or whichever low-budget effect you prefer). Refer to the following screenshot:

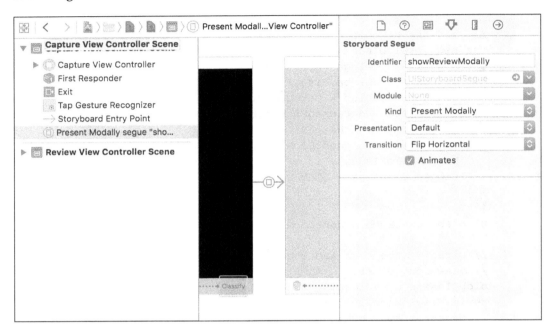

Detecting blobs against a plain background

Let's assume that the background has a distinctive color range, such as "cream to snow white". Our blob detector will calculate the image's dominant color range and search for large regions whose colors differ from this range. These anomalous regions will constitute the detected blobs.

> For small objects such as a bean or coin, a user can easily find a plain background such as a blank sheet of paper, plain table-top, plain piece of clothing, or even the palm of a hand. As our blob detector dynamically estimates the background color range, it can cope with various backgrounds and lighting conditions; it is not limited to a lab environment.

Create a new file, `BlobDetector.cpp`, for the implementation of our `BlobDetector` class. (To review the header, refer back to the *Defining blobs and a blob detector* section.) At the top of `BlobDetector.cpp`, we will define several constants that pertain to the breadth of the background color range, the size and smoothing of the blobs, and the color of the blobs' rectangles in the preview image. Here is the relevant code:

```
#include <opencv2/imgproc.hpp>

#include "BlobDetector.h"

const double MASK_STD_DEVS_FROM_MEAN = 1.0;
const double MASK_EROSION_KERNEL_RELATIVE_SIZE_IN_IMAGE = 0.005;
const int MASK_NUM_EROSION_ITERATIONS = 8;

const double BLOB_RELATIVE_MIN_SIZE_IN_IMAGE = 0.05;

const cv::Scalar DRAW_RECT_COLOR(0, 255, 0); // Green
```

Of course, the heart of `BlobDetector` is its `detect` method. Optionally, the method creates a downsized version of the image for faster processing. Then, we call a helper method, `createMask`, to perform thresholding and erosion on the (resized) image. We pass the resulting mask to the `cv::Canny` function to perform Canny edge detection. We pass the edge mask to the `cv::findContours` function, which populates a vector of contours, in the `vector<vector<cv::Point>>` format. That is to say, each contour is a vector of points. For each contour, we find the points' bounding rectangle. If we are working with a resized image, we restore the bounding rectangle to the original scale. We reject rectangles that are very small. Finally, for each accepted rectangle, we put a new `Blob` object in the output vector and optionally draw the rectangle in the original image. Here is the `detect` method's implementation:

```
void BlobDetector::detect(cv::Mat &image,
  std::vector<Blob> &blobs, double resizeFactor, bool draw)
{
  blobs.clear();

  if (resizeFactor == 1.0) {
    createMask(image);
  } else {
    cv::resize(image, resizedImage, cv::Size(), resizeFactor,
      resizeFactor, cv::INTER_AREA);
    createMask(resizedImage);
  }

  // Find the edges in the mask.
```

```
cv::Canny(mask, edges, 191, 255);

// Find the contours of the edges.
cv::findContours(edges, contours, hierarchy, cv::RETR_TREE,
  cv::CHAIN_APPROX_SIMPLE);

std::vector<cv::Rect> rects;
int blobMinSize = (int)(MIN(image.rows, image.cols) *
  BLOB_RELATIVE_MIN_SIZE_IN_IMAGE);
for (std::vector<cv::Point> contour : contours) {

  // Find the contour's bounding rectangle.
  cv::Rect rect = cv::boundingRect(contour);

  // Restore the bounding rectangle to the original scale.
  rect.x /= resizeFactor;
  rect.y /= resizeFactor;
  rect.width /= resizeFactor;
  rect.height /= resizeFactor;

  if (rect.width < blobMinSize || rect.height < blobMinSize) {
    continue;
  }

  // Create the blob from the sub-image inside the bounding
  // rectangle.
  blobs.push_back(Blob(cv::Mat(image, rect)));

  // Remember the bounding rectangle in order to draw it later.
  rects.push_back(rect);
}

if (draw) {
  // Draw the bounding rectangles.
  for (const cv::Rect &rect : rects) {
    cv::rectangle(image, rect.tl(), rect.br(), DRAW_RECT_COLOR);
  }
}
}
```

The `getMask` method simply returns the mask that we previously computed in the `detect` method:

```
const cv::Mat &BlobDetector::getMask() const {
  return mask;
}
```

The `createMask` helper method begins by finding the image's mean color and standard deviation using the `cv::meanStdDev` function. We calculate a range of background colors based on a certain number of standard deviations from the mean, as defined by the `MASK_STD_DEVS_FROM_MEAN` constant near the top of `BlobDetector.cpp`. We deem values outside this range to be foreground colors. Using the `cv::inRange` function, we map the background colors (in the image) to white (in the mask) and the foreground colors (in the image) to black (in the mask). Then, we create a square kernel using the `cv::getStructuringElement` function. Finally, we use the kernel in the `cv::erode` function to apply the erosion morphological operation to the mask. This has the effect of smoothing the black (foreground) regions, so that they swallow up little gaps that are probably just noise. Here is the relevant code:

```
void BlobDetector::createMask(const cv::Mat &image) {

  // Find the image's mean color.
  // Presumably, this is the background color.
  // Also find the standard deviation.
  cv::Scalar meanColor;
  cv::Scalar stdDevColor;
  cv::meanStdDev(image, meanColor, stdDevColor);

  // Create a mask based on a range around the mean color.
  cv::Scalar halfRange = MASK_STD_DEVS_FROM_MEAN * stdDevColor;
  cv::Scalar lowerBound = meanColor - halfRange;
  cv::Scalar upperBound = meanColor + halfRange;
  cv::inRange(image, lowerBound, upperBound, mask);

  // Erode the mask to merge neighboring blobs.
  int kernelWidth = (int)(MIN(image.cols, image.rows) *
    MASK_EROSION_KERNEL_RELATIVE_SIZE_IN_IMAGE);
  if (kernelWidth > 0) {
    cv::Size kernelSize(kernelWidth, kernelWidth);
    cv::Mat kernel = cv::getStructuringElement(cv::MORPH_RECT,
      kernelSize);
    cv::erode(mask, mask, kernel, cv::Point(-1, -1),
      MASK_NUM_EROSION_ITERATIONS);
  }
}
```

That is the end of the blob detector's code. As you can see, it uses a general-purpose and rather linear approach, unlike the face detector in *Chapter 4, Detecting and Merging Faces of Mammals*, which relied on many special cases in its search for human eyes, cat eyes, and so forth. While the face detector also performed the classification of human versus cat faces, we are now using a separate blob detector and blob classifier, and this separation of responsibilities enables us to keep each class's implementation relatively simple.

For completeness, note that the Blob class's constructors have straightforward implementations that copy the arguments. For the blob's image, we make a deep copy because the original may change. (Remember, the original may be a subimage in a frame of video, and after detection, we draw rectangles atop the frame of video.) Similarly, the getter and setter methods of Blob are self-explanatory. Create a new file, Blob.cpp, and fill it with the following implementation:

```cpp
#import "Blob.h"

Blob::Blob(const cv::Mat &mat, uint32_t label)
: label(label)
{
  mat.copyTo(this->mat);
}

Blob::Blob() {
}

Blob::Blob(const Blob &other)
: label(other.label)
{
  other.mat.copyTo(mat);
}

bool Blob::isEmpty() const {
  return mat.empty();
}
uint32_t Blob::getLabel() const {
  return label;
}
void Blob::setLabel(uint32_t value) {
  label = value;
}
const cv::Mat &Blob::getMat() const {
  return mat;
}
```

```
int Blob::getWidth() const {
  return mat.cols;
}
int Blob::getHeight() const {
  return mat.rows;
}
```

Classifying blobs by color and keypoints

Our classifier operates on the assumption that a blob contains distinctive colors, distinctive keypoints, or both. To conserve memory and precompute as much relevant information as possible, we do not store images of the reference blobs, but instead we store histograms and keypoint descriptors.

Create a new file, `BlobClassifier.cpp`, for the implementation of our `BlobClassifier` class. (To review the header, refer back to the *Defining blob descriptors and a blob classifier* section.) At the top of `BlobDetector.cpp`, we will define several constants that pertain to the number of histogram bins, the histogram comparison method, and the relative importance of the histogram comparison versus the keypoint comparison. Here is the relevant code:

```
#include <opencv2/imgproc.hpp>

#include "BlobClassifier.h"

#ifdef WITH_OPENCV_CONTRIB
#include <opencv2/xfeatures2d.hpp>
#endif

const int HISTOGRAM_NUM_BINS_PER_CHANNEL = 32;
const int HISTOGRAM_COMPARISON_METHOD = cv::HISTCMP_CHISQR_ALT;

const float HISTOGRAM_DISTANCE_WEIGHT = 0.98f;
const float KEYPOINT_MATCHING_DISTANCE_WEIGHT = 1.0f -
  HISTOGRAM_DISTANCE_WEIGHT;
```

Beware that the HISTOGRAM_NUM_BINS_PER_CHANNEL constant has a cubic relationship to the memory usage of BeanCounter. For each blob descriptor, we store a three-dimensional (BGR) histogram with HISTOGRAM_NUM_BINS_PER_CHANNEL^3 elements, and each element is a 32-bit floating point number. If the constant is 32, each histogram's size *in megabytes* is (32^3)*32/(10^6)=1.0. This is fine for a small set of reference descriptors. If the constant is 256 (the maximum number of bins for an 8-bit color channel), the histogram's size goes up to a whopping value of (256^3)*32/(10^6)=536.9 megabytes! This is unacceptable, given the memory constraints of an iOS application.

At best, in a high-end iOS device, one gigabyte of RAM might be available to each application. Conservatively, you should worry if your app's memory usage approaches 100 megabytes.

Remember that OpenCV's SURF implementation is in the xfeatures2d module, which is part of opencv_contrib. If opencv_contrib is available (as indicated by the WITH_OPENCV_CONTRIB preprocessor flag), we import the <opencv/xfeatures2d.hpp> header and use SURF. Otherwise, we use ORB. This selection also affects the implementation of the constructor of BlobClassifier. OpenCV provides factory methods for various feature detectors, descriptors, and matchers, so we simply have to use the right combination of factory methods for SURF with FLANN matching, or ORB with brute-force matching based on the Hamming distance. Here is the constructor's implementation:

```
BlobClassifier::BlobClassifier()
 : clahe(cv::createCLAHE())
#ifdef WITH_OPENCV_CONTRIB
 , featureDetectorAndDescriptorExtractor(
     cv::xfeatures2d::SURF::create())
 , descriptorMatcher(cv::DescriptorMatcher::create("FlannBased"))
#else
 , featureDetectorAndDescriptorExtractor(cv::ORB::create())
 , descriptorMatcher(
     cv::DescriptorMatcher::create("BruteForce-HammingLUT"))
#endif
{
}
```

The `update` method's implementation calls a helper method, `createBlobDescriptor`, and adds the resulting `BlobDescriptor` to a vector of reference descriptors:

```
void BlobClassifier::update(const Blob &referenceBlob) {
  referenceBlobDescriptors.push_back(
    createBlobDescriptor(referenceBlob));
}
```

The `clear` method's implementation discards all the reference descriptors, so that `BlobClassifier` reverts to its initial, untrained state:

```
void BlobClassifier::clear() {
  referenceBlobDescriptors.clear();
}
```

The implementation of the `classify` method relies on another helper method, `findDistance`. For each reference descriptor, `classify` calls `findDistance` to obtain a measure of dissimilarity between the query blob's descriptor and reference descriptor. We find the reference descriptor with the least distance (best similarity) and return its label as the classification result. If there are no reference descriptors, `classify` returns 0, the *unknown* label. Here is the implementation of `classify`:

```
void BlobClassifier::classify(Blob &detectedBlob) const {
  BlobDescriptor detectedBlobDescriptor =
    createBlobDescriptor(detectedBlob);
  float bestDistance = FLT_MAX;
  uint32_t bestLabel = 0;
  for (const BlobDescriptor &referenceBlobDescriptor :
      referenceBlobDescriptors) {
    float distance = findDistance(detectedBlobDescriptor,
      referenceBlobDescriptor);
    if (distance < bestDistance) {
      bestDistance = distance;
      bestLabel = referenceBlobDescriptor.getLabel();
    }
  }
  detectedBlob.setLabel(bestLabel);
}
```

The `createBlobDescriptor` helper method is responsible for calculating a normalized histogram and keypoint descriptors for `Blob` and using them to build a new `BlobDescriptor`. To calculate the (non-normalized) histogram, we use the `cv::calcHist` function. Among its arguments, it requires three arrays to specify the channels we want to use, the number of bins per channel, and the range of each channel's values. To normalize the resulting histogram, we divide by the number of pixels in the blob's image. The following code, pertaining to the histogram, is the first half of the implementation of `createBlobDescriptor`:

```
BlobDescriptor BlobClassifier::createBlobDescriptor(
  const Blob &blob) const
{
  const cv::Mat &mat = blob.getMat();
  int numChannels = mat.channels();

  // Calculate the histogram of the blob's image.
  cv::Mat histogram;
  int channels[] = { 0, 1, 2 };
  int numBins[] = { HISTOGRAM_NUM_BINS_PER_CHANNEL,
    HISTOGRAM_NUM_BINS_PER_CHANNEL,
    HISTOGRAM_NUM_BINS_PER_CHANNEL };
  float range[] = { 0.0f, 256.0f };
  const float *ranges[] = { range, range, range };
  cv::calcHist(&mat, 1, channels, cv::Mat(), histogram, 3,
    numBins, ranges);

  // Normalize the histogram.
  histogram *= (1.0f / (mat.rows * mat.cols));
```

Before computing the color histogram, we could adjust the white balance as we did in the project, CoolPig, in *Chapter 1, Setting Up Software and Hardware*. This additional step might make the descriptor more robust with respect to variations in lighting conditions. On the other hand, the iOS camera system already evaluates the white balance, so we might do better to trust its result (and not apply an additional step). Feel free to experiment.

Now, we must convert the blob's image to grayscale and obtain keypoints and keypoint descriptors using the `detect` and `compute` methods of `cv::Feature2D`. With the normalized histogram and keypoint descriptors, we have everything we need to construct and return a new `BlobDescriptor`. Here is the remainder of the implementation of `createBlobDescriptor`:

```
    // Convert the blob's image to grayscale.
    cv::Mat grayMat;
    switch (numChannels) {
      case 4:
        cv::cvtColor(mat, grayMat, cv::COLOR_BGRA2GRAY);
        break;
      default:
        cv::cvtColor(mat, grayMat, cv::COLOR_BGR2GRAY);
        break;
    }

    // Adaptively equalize the grayscale image to enhance local
    // contrast.
    clahe->apply(grayMat, grayMat);

    // Detect features in the grayscale image.
    std::vector<cv::KeyPoint> keypoints;
    featureDetectorAndDescriptorExtractor->detect(grayMat,
      keypoints);

    // Extract descriptors of the features.
    cv::Mat keypointDescriptors;
    featureDetectorAndDescriptorExtractor->compute(grayMat,
      keypoints, keypointDescriptors);

    return BlobDescriptor(histogram, keypointDescriptors,
      blob.getLabel());
}
```

The `findDistance` helper method performs histogram comparison using the `cv::compareHist` function, and keypoint matching using the `match` method of `cv::DescriptorMatcher`. Each of the resulting keypoint matches has a distance, and we sum these distances. Then, as an overall measure of distance between the two blob descriptors, we return a weighted average of the histogram distance and the total keypoint matching distance. Here is the relevant code:

```
float BlobClassifier::findDistance(
  const BlobDescriptor &detectedBlobDescriptor,
  const BlobDescriptor &referenceBlobDescriptor) const
{
  // Calculate the histogram distance.
  float histogramDistance = (float)cv::compareHist(
    detectedBlobDescriptor.getNormalizedHistogram(),
    referenceBlobDescriptor.getNormalizedHistogram(),
    HISTOGRAM_COMPARISON_METHOD);

  // Calculate the keypoint matching distance.
  float keypointMatchingDistance = 0.0f;
  std::vector<cv::DMatch> keypointMatches;
  descriptorMatcher->match(
    detectedBlobDescriptor.getKeypointDescriptors(),
    referenceBlobDescriptor.getKeypointDescriptors(),
    keypointMatches);
  for (const cv::DMatch &keypointMatch : keypointMatches) {
    keypointMatchingDistance += keypointMatch.distance;
  }

  return histogramDistance * HISTOGRAM_DISTANCE_WEIGHT +
    keypointMatchingDistance * KEYPOINT_MATCHING_DISTANCE_WEIGHT;
}
```

That is the end of the blob classifier's code. Again, we see that a single class can provide useful, general-purpose computer vision functionality without a terribly complicated implementation. Perhaps this is a Zen moment; our work has been a path to (some kind of) simplicity! Of course, OpenCV hides a lot of complexity for us in its implementations of histogram-related functions and keypoint-related classes, and in this way, the library offers us a relatively gentle path.

For completeness, note that the `BlobDescriptor` class has a straightforward implementation. Create a new file, `BlobDescriptor.cpp`, and fill it with the following bodies for a constructor and getters:

```
#include "BlobDescriptor.h"

BlobDescriptor::BlobDescriptor(const cv::Mat &normalizedHistogram,
const cv::Mat &keypointDescriptors, uint32_t label)
: normalizedHistogram(normalizedHistogram)
, keypointDescriptors(keypointDescriptors)
, label(label)
{
}

const cv::Mat &BlobDescriptor::getNormalizedHistogram() const {
  return normalizedHistogram;
}
const cv::Mat &BlobDescriptor::getKeypointDescriptors() const {
  return keypointDescriptors;
}
uint32_t BlobDescriptor::getLabel() const {
  return label;
}
```

Now, we have finished all the code for BeanCounter!

Using the application and testing the tough cases

Gather your collection of objects, run BeanCounter, and observe your classifier's successes and failures. Also, check whether the detector is doing a good job. For the best results, obey the following guidelines:

- Work in a well-lit area, such as a sunny room.
- Use a flat, white background, such as a clean sheet of paper.
- View one object at a time.
- Keep the iOS device stable. If necessary, use a tripod or other support.
- Ensure that the object is in focus. If necessary, tap the screen to focus.
- If the object is shiny, ensure that it does not catch reflections.

Under these ideal conditions, what is your classifier's accuracy? Use BeanCounter to save some images of objects, and then select a few of them to add to the Xcode project as reference images. Rebuild and repeat. By training the classifier, can you achieve an accuracy of 80%, 90%, or even 95%?

Now, break the rules! See how the detector and classifier perform under less-than-ideal conditions. The following subsections illustrate some cases where BeanCounter proves to be robust.

An unevenly-lit background

Sometimes, a combination of the lighting conditions and background material may create a shift in brightness between background regions. For example, in the following screenshots, the background is a wrinkled piece of paper:

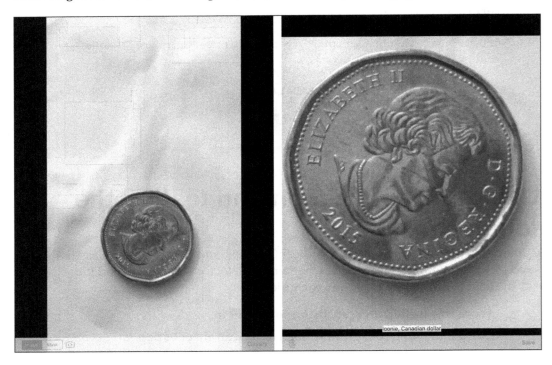

Here, the detector finds many small blobs that are really just subtle highlights and shadows around the wrinkles. Even so, the largest detected blob is the coin, which the classifier correctly labels as **loonie, Canadian dollar**.

The following screenshots illustrate a more extreme case. The background is the aluminum case of a laptop. Dim light comes from the laptop's screen and creates a gradient effect on the metallic surface:

Again, the detector finds many small blobs that are really just variations in lighting (and perhaps noise). The coin lies in a region where the light visibly starts to fall off. Nonetheless, the detector finds most of the coin, and the classifier produces the correct label, **Canadian nickel**. This is a good achievement for both the detector and classifier because we might expect them to struggle with the similar metallic colors of the coin and background.

Motion blur

If the user's hands are shaky or if the exposure is slow due to dim light, the image may suffer from motion blur. However, even with a noticeable amount of motion blur, the image may still yield useful keypoints. Moreover, the blur has no significant effect on the histogram. The following screenshot shows a nickel with motion blur:

Canadian nickel

Despite the moderately bad motion blur, the nickel's features are visible. BeanCounter displays the correct classification, **Canadian nickel**.

Out of focus

Sometimes, the camera fails to focus on the target. Then, the image may be too blurry to produce useful keypoints. However, again, the blur has little effect on the histogram. The following screenshot shows a loonie that is extremely out of focus:

Despite the poor autofocus result, the loonie is still classifiable because of its distinctive color. Within the limits of our classification set, it is the only object that is entirely gold-colored. BeanCounter correctly labels it **loonie, Canadian dollar**.

Of course, a bean is thicker than a coin. A bean may be out of focus while the background is in focus. Consider the following screenshot of a romano bean that is slightly out of focus:

romano bean

As usual, we see the distinctive colors of the bean and its bounced light. BeanCounter correctly reports that we are looking at a **romano bean**.

Reflection

Sometimes, a coin may catch the reflection of the iOS device, the user's hand, or another object. The reflection may create unusual variations in brightness or color—in other words, a distortion of the histogram. However, the reflection is unlikely to obscure the coin's keypoints and it may even help illuminate them. The following screenshot shows a reflection of my hand in a dime:

Canadian dime

Note the bright, pinkish region on the right-hand side of the dime. Despite this anomaly, BeanCounter produces a correct classification, **Canadian dime**.

Overlapping blobs

Sometimes, an object may be close to another object or to a disturbing element of the background. Then, the blob detector cannot crop out a lone object on a plain region of the background. Consider the following screenshots of a pinto bean near a toonie:

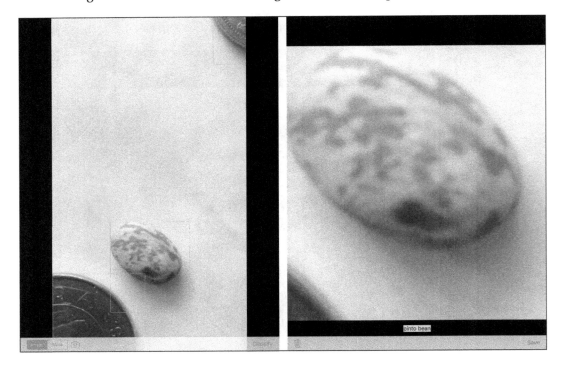

The detector has correctly cropped the bean and its bounced light. However, the rectangular crop also includes a corner of the toonie. Despite this extraneous element, the classifier produces the correct result, **pinto bean**.

The following screenshots show a more difficult case. The background contains text that intersects with the outline of a romano bean:

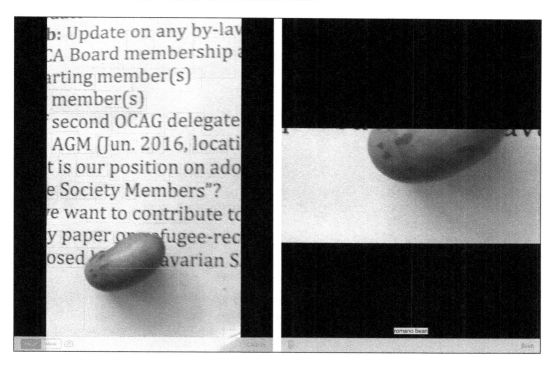

Here, the blob detector misses half of the bean, yet it detects the lower half and bounced light amid a plain white region of the background. Even based on this partial detection, the blob classifier produces the correct result, **romano bean**.

Taking your study of OpenCV to the next level

So far, you have learned several ways to control the camera, blend images, detect and classify objects, compare images, and apply geometric transformations. These skills can help you solve countless problems in your iOS applications.

Next, you might want to study a collection of advanced OpenCV projects. As of May 2016, there are no other books on OpenCV 3 for iOS. However, with your iOS skills, you can adapt code from any OpenCV 3 book that uses C++. Consider the following options from Packt Publishing:

- *OpenCV 3 Computer Vision Application Programming Cookbook, Third Edition*: This new edition will be published later in 2016. The book provides extensive coverage of OpenCV's C++ API with more than 100 practical samples of reusable code.

- *Learning Image Processing with OpenCV*: This book is a great choice if you are specifically interested in computational photography or videography. The projects use C++ and OpenCV 3.

- *OpenCV 3 Blueprints*: This book teaches a healthy mix of theory and practice, with tools and sample applications based on recent research and industry experience. Most of the projects use C++. You will also learn to develop Android apps using Android Studio, Java, and C++. Thus, you will expand your skill set to cover a second mobile platform!

Summary

This chapter has demonstrated a general-purpose approach to blob detection and classification. Specifically, we have applied OpenCV functionality to thresholding, morphology, contour analysis, histogram analysis, and keypoint matching.

You have also learned how to load and parse a PLIST file from an application's resource bundle. As Xcode provides a visual editor for PLIST files, they are a convenient way to configure an iOS app. Specifically, in our case, a configuration file lets us separate the classifier's training data from the application code.

We have seen that our detector and classifier work on different kinds of objects, namely beans and coins. We have also seen that the detector and classifier are somewhat robust with respect to variations in lighting, background, blur, reflections, and the presence of neighboring objects.

Finally, we have identified some further reading that may help you take your knowledge of computer vision and mobile app development to the next level.

This concludes our tour of iOS and OpenCV 3. Thank you for reading the book and for joining our informal community of computer vision learners! If you have any queries, you can visit the support site for my books at http://nummist.com/opencv, or feel free to contact me at josephhowse@nummist.com. I hope our paths will cross again in another book. Meanwhile, pick up your iPhone and go try some more visual experiments in this beautiful, sunlit world!

Index

hybrid images
  creating 76-81

I

immutable type 116
integrated development
      environment (IDE) 2
International Standards
      Organization (ISO) 33
iOS Developer Program
  URL 29
iOS Provisioning Portal
  URL 29
iPhoneography 30
ISO speed 33
iTunes Connect
  URL 29

K

kernel filter 79
keypoint matching
  about 149
  brute-force Hamming-distance
      matching 158
  defining 156
  FLANN 157
  ORB 158
  SURF 157

L

Lanczos 96
Landscape-right orientation 56
Laplacian edge-finding effect 80
Leningrad Optical Mechanical Association
      (LOMO) 31
lights
  setting up 36
LightWork
  alert, displaying 70
  blending controls, creating 81-86
  busy mode, starting 68
  busy mode, stopping 68
  camera requirement, specifying 45
  document copy, previewing 100, 101
  drawing copy, previewing 100, 101

executing 73
frameworks, adding 44
image, saving to Photos library 69
image, sharing via social media 71, 72
new object, previewing in scene 98-100
project, configuring 44
scene changes, viewing 97, 98
using 97
view controller, defining 46-50
view controller, laying out 46-50
view controller's implementation,
      expanding 90-96
view controller's interface, expanding 86-89
Linear Algebra Package (LAPACK) 12
local binary pattern histogram (LBPH) 106
Lomography 31

M

ManyMasks project
  building 146, 147
  configuring 114
  running, on iOS 146, 147
mask 149
model-view-controller (MVC) pattern 23
morphology 149

N

neighbors 105

O

object classification application
  planning 159-162
OpenCV
  defining 200
  references 157
  URL 3
OpenCV 3
  references, for documentation 30
OpenCV framework
  building, from source with
      extra modules 4-6
  extra modules, creating as optional 6
  prebuilt framework, obtaining with
      standard modules 3, 4
  setting up 3

www.ingramcontent.com/pod-product-compliance
Lightning Source LLC
Chambersburg PA
CBHW060551060326
40690CB00017B/3678